Photographers and artists: Thomas Arndt, Glen S. Axelrod, Dr. Herbert R. Axelrod, Bale and Danielsson, Cliff Bickford, Tom Caravaglia, Michael Defreitas, Isabelle Francais, R. Hanson, Fred Harris, Dieter Hoppe, Harry V. Lacey, P. Leysen, Ron and Val Moat, Mintern Brothers, A.J. Mobbs, Horst Müller, K.T. Nemuras, Paradise Park (Hawaii), Robert Pearcy, John R. Quinn, Elaine Radford, Routedale Agency, San Diego Zoo, Harald Schultz, Tony Silva, T. Tilford, Guy Van Den Bassche, A. Van Den Nieuwenhuizen, M. Vriends, R. Williams.

Distributed in the UNITED STATES by T.F.H. Publications, Inc., One T.F.H. Plaza, Neptune City, NJ 07753; in CANADA to the Pet Trade by H & L Pet Supplies Inc., 27 Kingston Crescent, Kitchener, Ontario N2B 2T6; Rolf C. Hagen Ltd., 3225 Sartelon Street, Montreal 382 Quebec; in CANADA to the Book Trade by Macmillan of Canada (A Division of Canada Publishing Corporation), 164 Commander Boulevard, Agincourt, Ontario M1S 3C7; in ENGLAND by T.F.H. Publications, PO Box 15, Waterlooville PO7 6BQ; in AUSTRALIA AND THE SOUTH PACIFIC by T.F.H. (Australia) Pty. Ltd., Box 149, Brookvale 2100 N.S.W., Australia; in NEW ZEALAND by Ross Haines & Son, Ltd., 82 D Elizabeth Knox Place, Panmure, Auckland, New Zealand; in the PHILIPPINES by Bio-Research, 5 Lippay Street, San Lorenzo Village, Makati, Rizal; in SOUTH AFRICA by Multipet Pty. Ltd., P.O. Box 35347, Northway, 4065, South Africa. Published by T.F.H. Publications, Inc. Manufactured in the United States of America by T.F.H. Publications, Inc.

The Professional's Book of
CONURES

A pair of Jandaya Conures (*Aratinga jandaya*).

JOHN COBORN

Petz's Conure (Aratinga canicularis).

Contents

Introduction
7

Housing
17

Feeding
35

General Care
43

Ailments and Diseases
53

Breeding
63

Hand-rearing
73

The Species
81

Conservation
137

Illustration Index
140

Index
141

Golden-crowned Conure (*Aratinga aurea*). Conures are often called "miniature Macaws."

Introduction

Conures are essentially Macaws in miniature, and anyone with the desire to own one of these large, spectacularly colored "kings" of the parrot world would do well to acquire some experience with their smaller relatives. This is not to say that Conures do not offer an attractive proposition for the would-be aviculturist in their own right. They have much to recommend them in terms of character and inquisitiveness, and they often possess a high degree of intelligence.

With their lively dispositions, individuals quickly become tame and will gain a great deal of confidence in their owner, provided they are treated with respect. Although their powers of mimicry are not as well developed as those of other South American parrots (notably Amazons), they will frequently learn to repeat a few words.

Petz's, or Orange-fronted, Conure enjoys great popularity as a cage bird, especially in the USA, although its potential in this respect is not so widely recognized among European enthusiasts. Nevertheless, the choice of subject for the would-be pet owner is quite a wide one, as any of the commonly imported species are suitable for training, provided they are obtained at a sufficiently early age. No adult bird will adapt to an existence as a caged pet with anything like the same degree of acceptance as a youngster which has known no other way of life.

By far the vast majority of Conures offered for sale will be wild-caught, as captive-breeding is still regarded as a remarkable achievement where most species are

"With their lively dispositions, individuals quickly become tame and gain a great deal of confidence in their owner, provided they are treated with respect."

Profile of a Cobalt-winged Parakeet (*Brotogeris cyanoptera*). In the past, this species was often confused with the Tovi Parakeet (*Brotogeris jugularis*).

Orange-flanked Parakeet (*Brotogeris pyrrhopterus*) perched among geraniums.

generations. Among the more prolific species are the Golden-crowned, Red-bellied, Green-cheeked and Petz's Conures, although lately Sun, Jandaya, and Dusky-headed Conures are proving themselves equally capable of emulating this reproductive success.

Some may regard the general lack of bright coloration displayed by many Conures as an impediment to their successful establishment as a foremost choice among breeders (most species are predominantly green). However, individual species, such as the Queen of Bavaria's, Patagonian and Jandaya, with their flamboyant appearances, more than make up for the shortcomings of their duller brethren. With its fiery yellow plumage, the Sun Conure is one of the most spectacular members of the parrot tribe, although only in flight is its true beauty revealed.

Generally, members of the *Aratinga* family are inclined to be more noisy and destructive than the group of *Pyrrhura* Conures, but all can be critcized for their loud,

concerned. However, there are those who welcome the extra challenge afforded by these neo-tropical Parakeets.

It is certainly pleasing to know that many specialist breeders, particularly in the USA, are producing youngsters in ever-increasing numbers and sometimes even to second and subsequent

screeching voices and the rapidity with which they will reduce any timber-work to mere matchwood.

Another point to be borne in mind is that they are superb escape artists and are adept at finding the smallest hole through which to squeeze and make their bid for freedom. Constant inspection of any enclosure housing Conures is advised. Never leave a small

A bevy of Petz's Conures (*Aratinga canicularis*) at an importer's compound.

"*Another point to be borne in mind is that they [Conures] are superb escape artists and are adept at finding the smallest hole through which to squeeze and make their bid for freedom.*"

A pair of bright Jandaya Conures (*Aratinga jandaya*). These colorful Conures are often more expensive than their duller brethren.

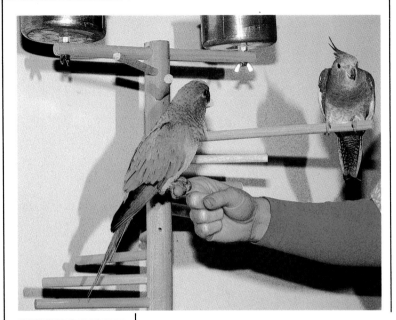

hole to be dealt with later, as the birds will undoubtedly attend to it in the shortest possible space of time—and not with a view to carrying out essential repairs!

Conures vary greatly in size, price, and availability. Members of the *Aratinga* group are generally far more readily available to aviculturists than the *Pyrrhuras* and are consequently less expensive. In captivity they invariably prove to be much more productive, with nests

Golden-crowned Conure (*Aratinga aurea*) with a Cockatiel (*Nymphicus hollandicus*).

A trio of psittacines: Jandaya Conure (*Aratinga jandaya*), Blue and Gold Macaw (*Ara ararauna*), and Scarlet Macaw (*Ara macao*).

containing seven or eight eggs not an uncommon occurrence.

On account of their greater availability, in this book I shall concentrate on the *Aratingas*, although the more widely obtainable members of the *Pyrrhura* genus will be featured, along with the single representative of the genus *Nandayus*, which is closely allied to the *Aratingas* and hardly justifies being afforded a separate generic term. The forms of the Patagonian Conure will be featured as representatives of the small *Cyanoliseus* genus.

In addition, the *Brotogeris* genus will be covered. Although not true Conures, they are found in similar habitats and their treatment in captivity is largely the same. Indeed, many birdkeepers mistakenly refer to them as Conures. Until two decades ago, literally hundreds of thousands were exported (especially White-wings, Canary-wings and Tovis)—mostly destined to become pets. Nowadays far fewer are allowed to depart from their native South America and they therefore command much higher prices.

Whichever species attracts one's initial attention, reader—beware! Keeping parrots of any type can become highly addictive, and with such interesting personalities as possessed by

A pair of Sun Conures (*Aratinga solstitialis*) will form a strong bond with one another.

"Whichever species attracts one's initial attention, reader—beware! Keeping parrots can become highly addictive . . ."

Psittacines. Conures thrive on constant companionship— either that of their owner in the case of pet birds, or that of others of their own kind.

Will their noisy outbursts prove unduly disturbing to neighbors? Does your garden or backyard afford sufficient space to permit aviaries to be sited as far away as possible from any situation where their occupants might cause a nuisance?

Remember, too, that all Conures have a habit of being extremely destructive and replacing timbers used in the construction of their quarters can be both a costly and time-

Artist's rendering of various Conures.

A pair of Queen of Bavaria's Conures (*Aratinga guarouba*).

many members of the Conure family, a single acquisition is unlikely to remain that way for very long!

As with any member of the parrot tribe, Conures can be very demanding of one's time, but those persons who are prepared to devote sufficient attention to their daily requirements will undoubtedly be richly rewarded in terms of companionship.

When considering the most suitable choice one should also contemplate whether he is the right type of owner for these engaging little

"Where any Conure is to be kept as a pet, the ideal ratio is one to one, i.e., no one should possess more than one pet."

consuming exercise.

With the constantly escalating prices commanded by these birds, individuals kept in unprotected aviaries may be considered extremely vulnerable to theft, so it may be necessary to arrange for certain security measures.

Where any Conure is to be kept as a pet, the ideal ratio is one to one, i.e., no one should possess more than one pet. Most pet parrots have an amazing propensity for jealousy and their passions may easily be inflamed by the acquisition of a second "rival" for their owner's affections. However, once "bitten by the bug," it is likely that few readers will be able to follow this advice.

Never embark on acquiring

A pair of adult male *Pyrrhura* Conures: Green-cheeked Conure (*Pyrrhura molinae*), and Red-bellied Conure (*Pyrrhura frontalis*).

your pet until you have a full understanding of its needs. In this respect you will require a good comprehension of its requirements with regard to housing, feeding, and general care. You will also find it desirable to possess at least a rudimentary knowledge of the treatment of the various ailments and diseases to which your pet may be prone.

If your aim is to take up the challenge of breeding these birds (and with the increasing restrictions on exportation, the more people who can be persuaded to do so, the better will be the chances of survival for many species), then you must learn something of their nesting habits and the extra requirements for feeding young. Only after all these aspects of husbandry have been taken into consideration should one decide upon the species to be kept.

Golden-crowned Conure (*Aratinga aurea*). This species has actually increased its habitat because of deforestation.

Dusky-headed Conure (*Aratinga weddellii*) and a Nanday Conure (*Nandayus nenday*).

Housing

Conures range in size from species measuring little more than 6 inches (15 cm) in total length to the Greater Patagonian Conure which exceeds 20 inches (53 cm) from its black bill to the tip of its olive-green and brown tail. It therefore is obvious that the size and type of accommodation will vary according to the species to be kept.

For the pet-bird keeper, a large selection of mostly excellently designed cages is available, primarily of all-wire construction, fitted with a sliding metal droppings tray and at least two feeding receptacles which are attached to the side of the cage.

Anyone wishing to purchase a suitable cage for his pet Conure is advised to visit a number of shops to gain a comprehensive idea of what is available. Always make a point of buying the largest cage which the size of your room and your wallet will allow. Horizontal dimensions are far more important than height, as although all Conures will clamber about their cage to a certain extent,

restricting their movement across the width of the cage will prove greatly more disadvantageous than confining their upward and downward progression.

Many cages are produced in vastly elaborate designs and in a variety of materials (brass ones can cost a great deal) and will serve as an attractive

Jandaya Conures (*Aratinga jandaya*) and Sun Conures (*Aratinga solstitialis*) in a housing set-up that is typical for breeding. Note the tubing for the automatic watering system.

Nanday Conure (*Nandayus nenday*) and a Red-masked Conure (*Aratinga erythrogenys*) perched atop a travelling cage.

"Conures have very strong beaks and are quite capable of cutting through wire which is of less than 16 g quality."

Opposite: Finsch's Conures (*Aratinga finschi*) and a pair of brotogerids in an outdoor aviary.

centerpiece for any room, even before the installation of their occupant. Nevertheless, for those on a limited budget, it is certainly not necessary to spend large sums of money on providing suitable accommodation.

In many respects a standard box-type cage, with three enclosed wooden sides and a punch-bar metal front, is a more satisfactory alternative. It helps to create a sense of security for its occupant and offers the distinct advantage that it is easily constructed by the average handyman.

A suitable cage for an average-sized Conure, say, the 10 inch (25 cm) Golden-crowned, would be one measuring 30 inches (76 cm) by 18 inches (46 cm) by 15 inches (38 cm). Cover the interior woodwork—particularly any protruding, easily accessible surfaces—with ½-inch (1.3 cm) welded mesh, to provide a "climbing frame" for your pet. You will then be combining the advantages of an all-wire cage with the more protected environment afforded by the wooden-sided cage.

The bars of the cage should be spaced no more than ½-inch (1.3 cm) apart or, if welded mesh is used, it should not be any larger than ½-inch (1.3 cm) square. Conures have very strong beaks and are quite capable of cutting through wire which is of less than 16 g quality.

Your cage must therefore be of robust construction and

there should be no loose or unsoldered wires on which your pet may injure itself. Remember, too, that most Conures are highly intelligent and may soon learn how to undo a simple catch—fitting a small padlock to the cage door is an excellent idea.

If your cage is of the type featuring a metal droppings

result in a certain amount of wear and tear over the years.

One can delay this natural process by always making sure that a thick floor covering is employed. In this respect there really is no more effective (or, indeed, cheaper) solution to the problem than installing sheets of newspaper. If one places a

A group of young Conures amusing themselves on their playground. Most Conures can utilize toys made for Cockatiels.

tray, make sure that the edges have not become rusted and worn, as any sharp protrusion can inflict damage to the bird's feet.

Usually this tray is the first part of the cage to show signs of deterioration, as constant scraping of its surface to remove excess accumulations of droppings will inevitably

number of layers in the cage at the same time, it is a simple matter to remove one on a daily basis, thereby ensuring a high standard of cleanliness at any given point.

Other alternatives for covering the floor of your Conure cage include sand sheets, loose sand, wood shavings and sawdust. All

"Remember . . . that Conures are highly intelligent and may soon learn how to undo a simple catch— fitting a small padlock to the cage door is an excellent idea."

have their disadvantages and, apart from the extra cost, they are not as readily available.

Sandsheets are generally manufactured to fit the standard pet Budgerigar cage and it may be necessary to install anything up to half a dozen to cover the floor of the cage in question. Besides, parrots enjoy nothing better than ripping them to shreds in the shortest possible time and their owner may be fighting a losing battle trying to maintain a clean and tidy flooring. Abrasive scraps will inevitably be deposited in the water pot, creating a soggy mess, and frequent cleaning operations will be generally necessitated by their use.

Sand can be purchased loose from your local pet shop (never use ordinary builder's sand). Although most Conure droppings are not of the most liquid variety, the birds do consume a reasonable quantity of fruit, ensuring that their excreta is not as solid as that of more exclusively seed-eating species. The mixture of loose sand and droppings can be a highly glutinous one, which can prove extremely difficult to remove from the metal tray.

A thick layer of wood shavings will absorb most of the liquid content of the birds' excreta, but make sure that the lumber mill from which they have been obtained is not merchandising wood which has been treated with any harmful chemicals. Shavings from stained timber may also mar your pet's plumage.

Sawdust is highly

unsuitable, as it is likely to blow about the room with every flap of the birds' wings. It can also be the cause of eye infections if tiny particles enter the retina. Again the fine powder will often clog up food and water pots.

Unfortunately, many of the containers specifically designated for use in parrot cages are totally unsuited to their purpose. While perfectly adequate for the smaller Grass Parakeets, Cockatiels, etc., the breakable plastic type will certainly not

Profile of a Golden-capped Conure (*Aratinga auricapilla*). This species is relatively rare in captivity.

withstand the rigors of an attack by the beak of a more powerful bird such as a Conure. The broken fragments of any containers destroyed in this manner may also prove hazardous to the bird. Galvanized metal or ceramic bowls lend themselves far better to the purpose. Ideally, the former should be used for the Conure's supply of seed and the latter employed for drinking water, as any chemical additives administered in liquid form may react with the metal, with possibly harmful effects.

You should supply food bowls which are at least twice the size of those fitted to the cage as standard, as the original ones are generally far too small to be practical and quickly become clogged with husks, sunflower seed shells, and other debris. The large metal hook-on type is quite satisfactory, although certain more mischievous pets may soon learn to unhook them, thus spilling their contents.

The provision of suitable perching must be afforded due consideration; the type

supplied with commercially manufactured parrot cages is woefully inadequate. Smooth wooden dowelling may be easy to fit and equally simple to remove for cleaning purposes but, being of one thickness throughout its length, it does not offer any exercise for the bird's feet and supplying nothing but this form of perch may be storing up future health problems.

Nowadays, some manufacturers have even taken to producing plastic perching, which is even less satisfactory. A diameter of at least 1 inch (2.5 cm) is suitable for Conures. Variation in width is best supplied in the form of short lengths of stout branches.

Instead of needing regular cleaning, these natural wooden perches can simply be thrown away once they become soiled. By this time

The Jandaya Conure (*Aratinga jandaya*) is a good candidate for the outdoor aviary, as it can withstand freezing temperatures (32°F, 0°C).

Jandaya Conure (*Aratinga jandaya*) on top of its wire cage. This species gets along with small birds such as Budgerigars.

"Whereas housing a single pet is a fairly simple matter, siting an aviary and choosing the most suitable items for its construction require a great deal more forethought."

your pet will have gained great enjoyment from gnawing away the bark, from which certain essential vitamins may be obtained. Providing rough natural perching will help to ensure that your Conure does not become prone to suffering sores on the pads of its feet.

It is perfectly safe to cut branches from a large variety of different trees for this purpose, but the best advice is to stick to common deciduous types (those which shed their leaves in winter), such as elm, ash, willow, etc. Make certain that branches are taken only from trees which have not been sprayed with insecticide or herbicide. Any branches cut from a fruit orchard are

particularly suitable. In the spring it is a good idea to offer the occasional sprig of hazel, which your pet will demolish with obvious relish.

Whereas housing a single pet is a fairly simple matter, siting an aviary and choosing the most suitable items for its construction require a great deal more forethought. Conures have been known to breed in suitably sized flight cages, but success is far more likely to be achieved if a pair is offered the sole occupancy of an outside aviary.

Such an enclosure need not necessarily be very large. Indeed, many pairs seem to positively welcome the added feeling of seclusion offered by a relatively small flight. It is not even essential for their aviary to be positioned to receive direct sunlight, as a well-shaded corner may provide the birds with a greater incentive to go to nest.

To some extent size will be dictated by the species to be kept. A minimum of 8–10 ft (2.4–3 m) is recommended for the smaller Conures, while the larger species, such as the Queen of Bavaria's and the Patagonians, will be happier if allocated a flying space of no less than 12–15 ft (3.6–4.5 m).

Conures, like all other neo-tropical parrots and parakeets, become extremely aggressive during the breeding season, and the golden rule is one pair per flight. Obviously, there are exceptions to every rule, and some breeders may achieve a fair measure of reproductive success with certain species kept on the colony system. Conures are very much individuals and there may be distinct behavioral differences between two pairs of the same species even when kept in exactly the same manner. Careful observation is the key to preventing undue squabbling.

The best advice is always to err on the side of caution. No two individuals will ever respond to a situation in the same way. Murderous intent is

"Conures, like all other neotropical parrots and parakeets, become extremely aggressive during the breeding season, and the golden rule is one pair per flight."

Nanday Conure (*Nandayus nenday*) and Red-masked Conure (*Aratinga erythrogenys*) engaged in a preening session.

by no means unheard of among members of the Conure family and even a short burst of pugnaciousness can result in disfigurement or the loss of a limb.

Out of the breeding season it is quite possible to house several individuals together. Indeed, when not rearing young, most Conures are extremely sociable birds and they will normally appreciate the company of others of their own species.

In the past, housing a large number within one enclosure

A pair of Queen of Bavaria's Conures (*Aratinga guarouba*) inside their aviary. The accommodations for this species must be virtually indestructible, as these Conures are notorious gnawers.

would serve as the best means of identifying a true pair, allowing the breeder to separate them from the main group to enable them to go to nest without disturbance. Nowadays, with the advent of surgical sexing, such means of distinguishing the sexes (most species are not sexually dimorphic) are no longer necessary.

Even if space is at a premium, it is never advisable to accommodate both *Aratinga* and *Pyrrhura* Conures in the same enclosure, as fighting will inevitably occur between the two genera. Where a range of flights is to be constructed, it is advisable to double-wire between adjoining quarters to prevent toes from being nipped and even beaks from being damaged if the wire mesh is of a sufficiently large size.

Welded mesh is recommended for use in the construction of any housing quarters intended for members of the Conure family. It is far more durable than ordinary wire-netting and although somewhat more costly, the extra initial expenditure will be more than adequately compensated over the ensuing years. Replacing wire-mesh cladding is extremely time-consuming and necessitates finding temporary alternate accommodation for the birds. Sizes of welded mesh vary from ½-inch (1.3 cm) square, through 1 inch by ½-inch (2.5 cm by 1.3 cm) to 1 inch (2.5 cm) square (other intermediate sizes may also be available),

A pair of Cactus Conures (*Aratinga cactorum*). These birds cannot tolerate cold temperatures or frost conditions.

Finsch's Conure (*Aratinga finschi*) munching on a leaf.

"Once fully acclimatized, all Conures are extremely hardy creatures and perfectly able to withstand the rigors of a winter in the northern hemisphere."

with the former being the most expensive.

Although all the above sizes will be quite sufficient to contain any Conure, the larger ones do not restrict the entry of vermin which may also introduce infectious diseases to your stock as well as vastly increasing one's food bills.

While the presence of mice may be deemed a nuisance, rats are another matter, as they are quite capable of killing a bird the size of a Conure and will wreak absolute havoc if they ever gain admittance to a nest-box. Their unimpeded passage must therefore be prevented at all costs.

Concrete flooring provides the only real answer to the problem. As Conures will rapidly destroy any vegetation planted in their flight, the use of concrete will not detract from the potential attractiveness of a naturally planted environment. If

possible, arrange the floor so that it incorporates a slight slope, with a drainage hole at the lowest point. In this way the floor can easily be hosed down from time to time, scrubbed clean with a stiff broom and doused with disinfectant as prevention against the spread of any infection.

Once fully acclimatized, all Conures are extremely hardy creatures and perfectly able to withstand the rigors of a winter in the northern hemisphere. In a warmer environment they may be inclined to go to nest outside of their normal breeding season.

One of the problems of preventing them from laying eggs during the colder months of the year is caused by the need to leave their nest-boxes in position throughout the year for roosting purposes. In the wild they will spend the night in tree cavities and this habit extends to an adaptation of this natural activity in captivity. It is therefore unnecessary to provide a fully enclosed shelter. Provided that the site of the aviary is a fairly sheltered one, an open-fronted shelter is perfectly adequate.

On account of its strident vocalization, no one with less than understanding neighbors should consider including the noisy Queen of Bavaria's in any collection of Conures. In terms of beak size and strength, there is very little difference between this species and the smaller Macaws; therefore, any

Left and below:
**Tovi Parakeets
(*Brotogeris
jugularis*), like
all brotogerids,
are active birds
that need
generous cages.**

enclosure intended to house
these birds will need added
protection if it is not to suffer
extensive damage to areas of
exposed timber framework.

Ideally, any flight intended
for the larger members of the
Conure family should be
constructed of a tubular metal
framework, covered with 12 or
14 gauge welded mesh or
chain-link netting. All
exposed timber surfaces
should be covered with sheet
metal and the ends of the
perches should be set into a
covering of the same material,

Finsch's Conure (*Aratinga finschi*). Natural branches help wear down the claws, exercise the muscles of the feet, and provide a chew for the parrots.

"A most satisfactory method of housing Conures and other parrots, which has become increasingly in vogue in recent years, is that of the suspended aviary."

to prevent the birds from chewing at the ends and causing the perches to collapse.

Some breeders make a point of surrounding the entrance to the nest-box with metal sheeting, but this is really rather unnecessary, giving way to a somewhat sterile receptacle which may not meet with the birds' approval. It does no harm to allow them to chew around the opening, although placing a sheet of metal in the base of the nest-box in such a way that the edges may be turned up and tacked to the sides is a good idea, as it will foil any attempts by the nesting pair to chew through the base with the result that eggs and/or young are unceremoniously deposited on the ground.

A most satisfactory method of housing Conures and other parrot species, which has become increasingly in vogue in recent years, is that of the suspended aviary. It is basically an all-wire cage, containing a shelter and nest-box of suitable dimensions, the floor of which is situated 3–4 ft (91 cm–1.2 m) above the ground. Among its advantages over a more conventional type of housing is the fact that droppings and other debris simply fall through the wire floor and it is an easy matter to clear away accumulated deposits without having to enter the flight. If a pair is engaged in nesting operations, the level of disturbance is kept to a minimum.

In addition, these structures are quick, easy, and relatively inexpensive to build and there is far less chance of vermin being able to take up residence. Infestations of parasitic worms are less likely to occur, as the occupants of such an enclosure do not have the opportunity of becoming re-infested. This type of accommodation has enjoyed much greater popularity in the USA than in Europe, but there are signs that European aviculturists are becoming aware of the advantages of housing their birds in such a labor-saving manner.

Naturally, no method of providing accommodation is without its disadvantages, and the main inherent fault with such a system is that the appearance of these pens is not generally as attractive as the more conventional type of aviary design. Another point to be borne in mind is that

Conures do enjoy spending a certain amount of time on the ground, scratching around for tidbits, a pastime that is denied to them when occupying one of these suspended aviaries.

No matter how much accommodation one has at one's disposal, it is highly unlikely that it will ever be sufficient. Once having acquired a pair of Conures, there will undoubtedly be a desire to obtain another and, from then on, their owner is well and truly "hooked."

Therefore, it always pays to plan ahead, as there will be a constant need to expand the number of enclosures available. If a range of flights is constructed in sectional panels, the task of removing a side wall to add to the number of pens will be made that much easier. Built in this way, it will also be possible to dismantle the whole structure at any time for removal purposes.

Aviary panels can be purchased ready-made, usually in standard 6 ft by 3 ft (1.8 m by 91 cm) sections. Generally three types are marketed: an all-wire panel which may be clad in various sizes and gauges of wire-mesh, wooden sections for the

Nanday Conures (*Nandayus nenday*). In the wild, these birds live in savannahs and palm groves; they feed on the ground under palm trees that have dropped their seeds.

Blue-crowned Conure (*Aratinga acuticaudata*). Members of this species actively and frequently engage in social preening.

construction of housing quarters and a wire panel incorporating a door.

Flight doors should be no more than 4 ft (1.2 m) in height, as most birds will occupy the higher reaches of the enclosure and there is less chance of would-be escapees making a bid for freedom if the door height is restricted in this manner.

One should always aim to enter the aviary on as few occasions as possible and in this respect the inclusion of a feeding hatch is extremely desirable. Some species can become aggressive towards their owner as well as to other birds while they have chicks in the nest.

In the case of a newly introduced pair, it is a wise precaution to provide two separate feeding stations, as the dominant half of a would-be partnership may well attempt to prevent its prospective mate from feeding.

A wholesome, varied diet is one of the first essentials for the well-being of any creature to be kept in captivity. By and large, Conures are not fastidious feeders. *Pyrrhuras* will readily sample anything on offer, although members of the *Aratinga* group may prove a little more reticent about experimenting with new foods. It is therefore necessary to consider the varied selection of items for various conures.

A pair of fiery Sun Conures (*Aratinga solstitialis*).

Your local pet shop will have a wide variety of seed mixtures and feed dishes from which to choose.

Feeding

Conures should be provided with as varied a diet as possible. Supplying nothing other than seed and water will ensure that they do not starve, but is akin to forcing a human to exist on a diet of bread and water.

Individuals may prove reluctant to try out certain foods, but persevere and they can usually be persuaded to at least sample all manner of fruit and vegetables in addition to their staple seed diet. However, it is always a good idea to enquire of the seller as to the exact nature of the food to which a bird has become accustomed and to do one's best to simulate previous feeding methods during the initial stages of introduction to the new owner's routine.

Unfortunately, some birds will choose to starve rather than sample foods to which they are unaccustomed. Millet sprays are a great treat for many species of cagebirds, including Conures; an obstinate feeder can often be inveigled by the provision of this tidbit—especially if it has been soaked for 24–48 hours.

Offering a staple parakeet

mixture can prove extremely wasteful; all Conures will have their likes and dislikes and any constituent part falling under the latter category will simply be scattered in the process of searching through the mixture for the more favored items.

Perhaps the best method of establishing individual preferences is to provide all the different elements in the seed mixture in separate dishes—at least during the initial stages immediately following acquisition. A quick

"Unfortunately, some birds will choose to starve rather than sample foods to which they are unaccustomed."

Finsch's Conure (*Aratinga finschi*). Safe greenfood is an important part of the Conure diet.

In the wild, Petz's Conure (*Aratinga canicularis*) is frequently found dining on the fruit of fig trees. Sometimes this species will dine on insects and their larvae.

"While the oil-rich seeds . . . are particularly beneficial in terms of providing extra winter warmth, their provision must be strictly limited, as they are extremely fattening . . ."

check on consumption will soon reveal which types of seed are being regularly partaken. In the past it was incorrectly assumed that sunflower seed could be relied upon to form the large part of any parrot-like bird's diet. Although this item has always been a firm favorite among the vast majority of species, it cannot form the basis of a properly balanced diet on its own.

Those seeds which should be offered to your newly acquired Conure include canary, white millet, hemp, niger, linseed, oats and buckwheat—the latter two are perhaps the least likely to meet with approval. However, even if consumed in small quantities, their inclusion adds essential variety to your bird's diet. Peanuts can also be offered, but never the salted variety.

While the oil-rich seeds such as hemp and linseed are particularly beneficial in terms of providing extra winter warmth, their provision must be strictly limited, as they are extremely fattening and the former has been cited as the cause of developing liver complaints.

Soaking adds enormously to the nutritional value of a whole variety of seeds. Among those most suited to its purpose are sunflower and mung beans, both of which will be relished by practically all Conures. Soak the seed for 48 hours (24 may be sufficient during periods of warm weather). It should then be rinsed thoroughly under a running tap and drained of any excess water. Always provide soaked seed in a separate utensil and never leave it to become moldy—not that most Conures will leave it alone for sufficient time for it to do so!

Soaked sunflower seed is relished at any time of the year, but it is a particularly valuable medium for the successful rearing of youngsters. There is even greater value to be found in sprouted seed, particularly with regard to vitamin content. Ideally it should be allowed to grow to no more than ¼–inch (0.6 cm) in length, as it tends to develop a slightly sour taste once it exceeds that stipulation and will not be so readily consumed by your Conures. Commercial seed sprouters are available to produce the food in this highly digestible form, but a simple colander will suffice.

It is only comparatively recently that parrot specialists have become aware of the nutritional value of mung beans (obtainable at most health food stores). These small green-colored beans usually take a day or so longer to sprout than sunflower seed. Their protein and amino acid content is much higher than that of the majority of vegetables, and once they have acquired the taste for them, most Conures become addicted!

Invariably Conures can be persuaded to sample a variety of greenfoods, both wild and cultivated forms. Seeding grasses are particularly relished. It does no harm to offer them complete with roots and earth attached, as

"Soaked sunflower seed is relished at any time of the year, but it is a particularly valuable medium for the successful rearing of youngsters."

A pair of Mitred Conures (*Aratinga mitrata*). These Conures often raid grain crops in their native habitat.

Sprouted seed with fruit and vegetables. Note the variety of food types in this "salad."

One example of sprouting mix. The seed will sit for 24 to 48 hours, being stirred a few times a day to prevent spoilage and mold. Once the seeds begin to sprout, they are ready to be given to the birds.

these will be just as readily picked over in the search for tasty tidbits. If no other form of greenfood is available, simply dig up a piece of turf and offer it intact; you will be surprised how much enjoyment will be gained from such a simple expedient.

As far as wild foods are concerned, there is no limit to the number and variety which can be offered for the consumption of your Conures. If they refuse to try a certain

item, simply provide an alternative. Chickweed is a perennial favorite among all numbers of cagebirds, and Conures are no exception. Other choice items include groundsel, shepherd's purse and young dandelion leaves; many a Conure will sell its soul for the golden-yellow flower of a dandelion.

Cultivated greens such as kale, spinach, beet, lettuce, chicory, and celery tops are greatly appreciated. Peas in the pod can be offered, and small pieces of corn-on-the-cob are regarded as a great delicacy by most Conures. When cut into lengths of no more than 1 inch (2.5 cm), a great deal of unnecessary waste can be eliminated. Similar sized segments of carrot and celery may also meet with approval.

Feeding a large collection of Conures can be a costly undertaking, if for no other reason than the fact that, like all parrots, they are extremely wasteful feeders. Often only a single bite will be taken before the item of food is discarded. It is therefore advisable to dice any items of fruit or vegetables into one or two bite-sized portions.

Segments of apple, grapes and cherries will be eagerly accepted by most Conures. *Pyrrhuras* have a particular liking for fruit and will readily sample virtually any item offered; iron-rich pomegranate is a special favorite.

Soft fruits such as raspberries, black currants, gooseberries, red currants

"The food value of such everyday items as mashed potato, scrambled or hard-boiled egg, cheese, brown bread and milk, and various cereals should not be overlooked."

and blackberries can be included on the menu, although the juice of the latter may be responsible for staining the plumage— particularly noticeable in species such as the brilliant yellow Sun Conure. Remember that fruits and vegetables may prove equally acceptable in cooked form, rather than always being offered raw.

The food value of such everyday items as mashed potato, scrambled or hard-boiled egg, cheese, brown bread and milk, and various cereals should not be overlooked.

Even if your Conures refuse to sample something on first offering, there is no harm in trying it out again at a later date. Parrots can be fickle creatures and what may not be to their liking on one occasion may subsequently be greeted with unqualified approval. Similarly, they may suddenly decline a particular food for no apparent reason.

Although some individuals may accept small amounts of soaked monkey chow or soaked dog biscuits, few pelleted foods (even those formulated especially for feeding parrots) will even be sampled.

Orange-flanked Parakeet (*Brotogeris pyrrhopterus*). In the wild, members of this species consume fruit, corn, and various berries.

"On inspection, kernels should appear plump, with a high gloss finish to denote cleanliness."

It may be possible to encourage the more conservative feeders to try out different foods by withholding known favorites until later on in the day. Similarly, if one is unsure whether newly fledged youngsters are capable of fending for themselves, simply withhold all food for a period of two or three hours. No harm will befall them, but once this amount of time has elapsed, they will be sufficiently hungry to flock to the food pots, and it is an easy matter to ascertain which, if any, are incapable of feeding.

When purchasing seed, it is far less costly to do so in bulk. Buy the various types separately rather than in a mixture, which may contain several constituents which are not enjoyed by your Conures and which will otherwise be wasted. In this way it is also possible to prepare slightly

different staple diets for the various species in one's care.

Always buy your seed from a reputable supplier, remembering that the level of cleanliness is paramount in ensuring that you obtain the best possible quality available. Any seed which contains more than a very tiny percentage of dust is simply not worth buying.

Seed is grown in just about every part of the world and, like wine, quality may vary from region to region and according to the variation in the seasons. It therefore pays to maintain a constant quality control check, switching to an alternative source of supply as necessary. As a rule, crops grown in the more highly mechanized countries of the USA, Canada, Australia, etc., tend to be cleaner than those produced under the less highly automated conditions prevalent in the African states.

On inspection, kernels should appear plump, with a high gloss finish to denote cleanliness. Seed should never be stored for more than three or four months at a time and on no account should you offer any seed which has become moldy. Allowing a small sample of your seed to germinate provides an excellent guide to freshness—any in which a large proportion fails to sprout is undoubtedly stale and is therefore not of sufficient nutritional value to feed to your Conures.

Not all breeding Conures will partake of grit, so a

supply of cuttlefish bone must be available at all times to ensure that the intake of calcium is sufficient to prevent the production of soft-shelled eggs.

Nowadays a large variety of vitamin and mineral supplements are available commercially, but care should be taken in their application. The overzealous addition of a liquid vitamin solution to the drinking water, for example, can prove far more detrimental to the birds' health than its complete absence from the staple diet. Basically, if your Conures are receiving a richly varied selection of foods, there should be no need to supplement their nutritional intake in this way.

Conures are highly intelligent and will soon learn at what time of the day they are to be fed and will then pursue their owner with a watchful eye in an attempt to

ascertain which extra tidbits might be featured on the menu.

Offering treats in the form of small pieces of fruit or individual sunflower seeds may help in teaching a bird to adopt a greater degree of trust towards its owner during the initial stages following acquisition. Similarly, if it is necessary to administer liquid medicines at any time, a small amount can be concealed on a piece of fruit. Catching a bird to carry out an enforced oral administration can be extremely stressful, and such actions are to be avoided wherever possible. Avoiding stress is an important factor in ensuring good general care.

Finsch's Conure (*Aratinga finschi*). A healthy diet will go a long way toward keeping your Conure happy and healthy.

"Offering treats . . . may help in teaching a bird to adopt a greater degree of trust towards its owner during the initial stages following acquisition."

A pair of Jandaya Conures (*Aratinga jandaya*). If you keep more than one Conure, be sure each is getting enough to eat.

Green Conure (*Aratinga holochlora*). This species enjoys feeding on half-ripe mimosa seeds and on rice and corn.

General Care

Conures are no different in terms of their general care requirements than any other parrots, and affording them the right environment and day-to-day management is largely a matter of common sense.

Although Conures hail from the South American neo-tropics, it is not imperative to keep them in artificially heated quarters. Indeed, many will fail to thrive if maintained in an over-hot atmosphere.

Once fully acclimatized, they do not require heat, provided that they have access to draft-free accommodation. Conures are perfectly able to withstand low temperatures; what they cannot tolerate is a combination of cold and damp. Most will take to roosting in a nest-box if one is available, and this should be positioned at the highest point within the enclosure.

Although a centrally heated environment will not prove harmful to the well-being of a pet Conure, the resultant dry atmosphere can cause its plumage to suffer a certain lackluster appearance. Happily this shortcoming is easily alleviated by shooting your Conure with water from a fine mist sprayer of the type generally available for house plants.

Ideally, a light misting should be undertaken at least two or three times a week. Your pet will soon become accustomed to this process and many will actually grow to look forward to it. In an open flight all Conures will be seen sitting outside from time to time in the event of a light shower of rain, and this activity can easily be simulated in the home.

After a few dousings, most

"Conures are perfectly able to withstand low temperatures; what they cannot tolerate is a combination of cold and damp."

Many Conures enjoy a light shower of water a few times a week; additionally, as you can see here, some brotogerids actually like taking a real bath!

Nanday Conure (*Nandayus nenday*) chewing on its chain. Sturdy parrot chains for climbing—and chewing—are available at your local pet shop.

"Any Conure which is afforded plenty of attention from the outset will quickly lose its fear of humans and many of them can become unusually tame . . ."

pet Conures will open their wings in ecstasy at the prospect of this treatment. Never spray your pet too late in the evening when it may be forced to go to roost with its plumage still damp. On a particularly cold day it may be advisable to position the bird next to a radiator to dry. Do not place its cage immediately on top of a radiator and do not position it immediately in front of an open fire where the degree of heat may be too intense.

Ordinarily the cage should be placed in the most lived-in room in the house, where your pet will be subject to the greatest amount of companionship. If a bird is initially nervous, do not continually walk around its cage. Instead place it in a quiet corner, where it may

develop a greater sense of security. Small children, as well as other pets, should be kept at bay until the bird has had the chance to settle.

Never place the cage in direct sunlight or near the window where its occupant may be subjected to drafts. Under normal circumstances it should not be necessary to cover the bird at night, but if a particularly noisy party or other loud activity is in progress, it is wise to do so.

Any Conure which is afforded plenty of attention from the outset will quickly lose its fear of humans and many of them can become unusually tame, allowing themselves to be handled and possibly learning to mimic their owner's voice. In view of their mischievous behavior, they should be let out of their

cage only under strict supervision. Any bird which feels that it is not receiving due attention is capable of lengthy outbursts of high-pitched shrieking. A non-vocal Conure is usually a sick one.

Like all parrots, Conures can be extremely sensitive and may react badly to being transported from one set of surroundings to another. Allow your pet sufficient time to settle down before making any attempt to gain its

confidence. Patience must prevail.

Many newly imported Conures will have their wings clipped and it may be some months before they regain their full power of flight. Whether it is advisable to continue to snip the primaries on one wing as they grow is a matter of conjecture.

A fully-winged Conure can be extremely strong in flight and may be difficult for its owner to recapture once it has

Above and below: **Demonstration of wing-clipping. Many experts feel that clipping only one wing is the better method of restriction, as this way the bird cannot control the direction of its flight.**

Orange-flanked Parakeet (*Brotogeris pyrrhopterus*). Once your pet becomes tame it may enjoy having its head scratched.

Cobalt-winged Parakeet (*Brotogeris cyanoptera*). Teaching any parrot to talk takes a great deal of patience and perseverence.

been allowed out of its cage. On the other hand, clipping the wing feathers may prevent a much-loved pet from making a successful bid for freedom through a door or window which has inadvertantly been left open. Unfortunately, such occurrences are not uncommon.

Flight prevention may be regarded as cruel, although it may be simply a matter of "better safe than sorry." Whatever the pros and cons, the decision must rest with the owner and his or her personal circumstances.

While most young Conures are capable of learning to repeat a few words, their ability to mimic the human voice (or any other sound) is entirely unpredictable. In spite of the frequent appearance of dealers' notices to that effect, there is no such thing as a "guaranteed" talking parrot of any kind. Some may learn to repeat a single word and then never extend their education any further. If you are

determined to own a talking Conure, then the only certain way of doing so is to buy one which has already been taught to talk and which has exercised its full vocabulary in the presence of the intended purchaser. Such highly talented individuals are very rarely offered for sale.

Always be suspicious of the vendor offering an established pet for sale. His reasons for disposing of the bird may be perfectly genuine. On the other hand, his motives may not be so exemplary.

The fact that one person has failed to train a particular individual does not necessarily mean that any subsequent owner will be similarly unsuccessful, but the chances of achieving the desired results with an older bird, which has not proved itself tractable in the hands of its initial owner, must, at best, be considerably reduced. Buy a young, untrained bird and at

least you know that you are not trying to succeed where others have failed.

When training a young Conure to mimic, always start off with a single word or short phrase such as "Hello" or "Good morning." Be prepared to spend a great deal of time with the bird, repeating the same expression over and over again. Do not attempt to teach it a second phrase until it has mastered the first.

It is essential to develop a good relationship with any bird in training. One which has not learned to trust its owner will never develop the powers of mimicry. Using a tape recorder can provide a handy "back-up" service, but there is nothing to beat the personal contact of the human voice.

Try to exclude television and radio sounds in the background when attempting to train your pet. It is best if only one person in the family acts as a tutor, so that the young Conure learns to recognize the sound of only one voice. Some birds may prefer to listen to a male voice, while others may associate better with a female one. Be prepared to adapt to your pet's preferences rather than expect it to alter its natural inclinations to suit you.

Conures will seldom learn to repeat more than a few phrases. Their vocabulary is never likely to emulate that of an African Grey or an Amazon Parrot. Be content that your pet has learned to accept you as its friend and provider and

if it eventually comes to repeat the odd word or two, regard this as a bonus.

It is often the keeping of a single pet bird that leads to its owner making the progression from pet owner to bird-keeper and aviculturist. Once the appetite has been whetted to extend one's range of knowledge and the number of species kept, it inevitably becomes impractical to maintain a large stock as individual caged pets indoors.

One's thoughts must then turn to the construction of aviaries.

Housing a number of Conures in outside flights as opposed to indoors presents its own problems. Remember that your birds will have to be looked after summer and winter, 365 days a year. Attending to a dozen or more aviaries during a raging snowstorm or in a heavy downpour of rain can soon become a chore rather than a pleasurable pursuit.

Cobalt-winged Parakeet (*Brotogeris cyanoptera*). Once tame, your pet will enjoy supervised periods of freedom outside of its cage.

"Conures will seldom learn to repeat more than a few phrases. Their vocabulary is never likely to emulate that of an African Grey or an Amazon Parrot."

"A hospital cage should be available for the benefit of any bird which may fall sick, or which may simply be suffering the effects of the cold, shortened winter days."

Opposite: Artist's rendering of a trio of Golden-capped Conures (*Aratinga auricapilla*).

Such a task may prove even more irksome for those who have to go out to earn a living, leaving home during the winter when it is still dark and not returning in the daylight.

In such circumstances all due thought must be given to the problems of attending to the needs of one's collection. Not everyone is fortunate enough to have a partner who is prepared to take on the responsibility, and even then, holiday time and periods of sickness must be taken into account. Someone will have to attend to the birds' requirements at all times.

Certainly there are measures which can be undertaken to make life easier for the owner of a collection of aviary birds. A source of electricity supplied to the birdroom or the service passage between flights will be of enormous benefit.

Ideally any lighting system should be fitted with a dimmer switch, so that it is not necessary to plunge the birds into sudden darkness once their care has been attended to.

A hospital cage should be available for the benefit of any bird which may fall sick, or which may simply be suffering the effects of the cold, shortened winter days.

It is vitally important to inspect your birds at least twice a day, especially during the winter, when chills are most likely to occur. Sick birds succumb very quickly and many a fancier has regretted leaving matters one more day, in the hope that the individual concerned is simply feeling "a little under the weather." Invariably he will have the task of burying a corpse by the next morning.

It is also very important to ensure that your birds seek a

Orange-flanked Parakeet (*Brotogeris pyrrhopterus*) getting a health check. Whether you keep one Conure or one hundred, good care is essential for the bird's survival.

Red-bellied Conure (*Pyrrhura frontalis*). Members of this species use the nest box all year long.

suitable site for roosting each night. Conures kept in outside aviaries throughout the winter *must* have access to a nest-box to retire to at dusk. If the entrance hole is fitted with a flap which drops down by means of a device that can be operated from some distance away from the aviary, so much the better. Individuals can then be trapped in the nest-box and thus can be caught up at any time, without the need for their owner to dash around the flight madly wielding a catch-net and causing a great deal of stress among the occupants.

A good quality catch-net is, however, an essential piece of equipment. It should have a well-padded rim to avoid inflicting damage to the bird being caught. Remember that any bird being trapped in this manner is likely to object most strenuously to the

A pair of well-tamed brotogerids: a Cobalt-winged Parakeet (*Brotogeris cyanoptera*) and an Orange-flanked Parakeet (*Brotogeris pyrrhopterus*), the squawker.

indignity, and Conures have very powerful beaks with which to express their indignation; they are quite capable of inflicting quite a severe bite even when enclosed within the folds of a net.

A black or dark-colored catch-net is recommened, as it is less likely to cause alarm than a white or light-colored one. If you must resort to catching your subject while it is clinging to the wire mesh, be careful to disentangle its beak and claws before allowing it to drop into the folds of the net. If possible, it is far safer to catch a bird in flight. One occasion when it will be necessary to capture your Conure is when medical treatment is required.

". . . Conures have very powerful beaks with which to express their indignation; they are quite capable of inflicting quite a severe bite even when enclosed within the folds of a net."

Queen of Bavaria's Conure (*Aratinga guarouba*) preening itself. Regular preening should not be confused with feather-plucking, a dread habit of some parrots.

Ailments and Diseases

Conures do not make good patients for the simple reason that, as with all parrots, their ailments are difficult to identify and, therefore, one can never be sure that one is administering the right course of treatment. So many illnesses display exactly the same symptoms that correlating them with a particular line of treatment can often prove impossible. Unfortunately, only when the patient has died and a postmortem examination can be carried out can there be any certainty that the keeper was offering the best possible chance of a cure and then, of course, it is too late.

Among the most typical signs that all is not well are a general lack of activity and a loss of appetite. The bird may seem unhappy, perching with its eyes closed and feathers ruffled for long periods. A sick bird will stand with both feet firmly placed on the perch and its head may be tucked into the feathers of the back. Very often there is a change in the appearance of the droppings, which may become greenish in color and of a far more liquid

consistency than normal. Possibly there will be a discharge from the eyes or nostrils.

Loose droppings in themselves are not necessarily indicative of ill health. Any Conure which has consumed a reasonably large quantity of fruit is likely to suffer from loose bowel movements. Do not withhold a daily ration of fruit simply because of the state of the bird's excreta.

A gathering of Nanday Conures (*Nandayus nenday*). Note the bird with its head tucked under its wing; this posture is often a sign that something is wrong.

"Maintaining the patient at a constant 81°F (27°C) for a short period will often be sufficient to effect a cure, provided that the condition is not a serious one."

The first requirement of any ailing bird is heat, and in this respect a hospital cage should be regarded as an essential piece of equipment. Maintaining the patient at a constant 81°F (27°C) for a short period will often be sufficient to effect a cure, provided that the condition is not a serious one.

Unfortunately, the purchase of a hospital cage is seldom high on the list of priorities of the newcomer to the hobby of birdkeeping. Just as few people maintain an adequate emergency supply of medicaments, the prevalent attitude among those who keep parrots seems to be "wait until the day," which usually sees them rushing around trying to purchase a hospital cage or borrowing one from a fellow enthusiast. Most of these specially designed emergency care cages can be bought relatively inexpensively, and if their acquisition is responsible for saving one life, then it is surely money well spent.

Some may believe that simply placing the affected bird beside an intense source of heat will be an adequate cure in the case of illness, but such a course of action is seldom satisfactory. It is essential to be able to control the source of heat by means of a regulated thermostat of the type which is a standard feature in all hospital cages. Once the patient has begun to make a recovery, it will need a localized heat source, and this is where an infra-red light will be required, as the bird can move closer to or away from the heat as it desires.

As soon as the ailing bird is on the mend, the temperature

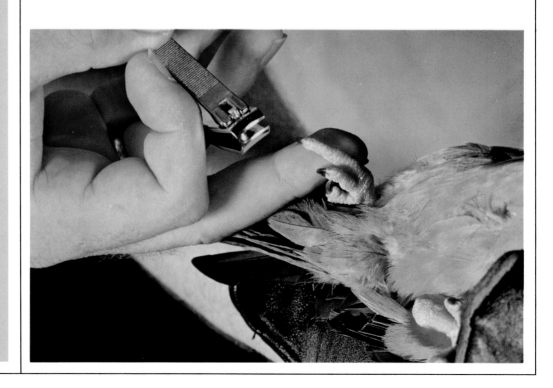

Nanday Conure (*Nandayus nenday*) getting its claws trimmed. This procedure should be done on a regular basis.

at which it has been maintained can be gradually reduced to that of the surrounding environment. In winter, owing to the great discrepancy between temperatures indoors and outdoors, it may not be feasible to return the bird immediately to its outside quarters. It may therefore be necessary for the owner to offer some form of temporary accommodation indoors until the advent of the first spell of warm weather.

Conures often form strong pair bonds, and the recovery of the ailing half of a partnership may be greatly speeded if it can remain within sight and sound of its mate, provided that it is not suffering from any infectious disease.

One of the most common superficial problems among Conures and their allies is that of a damaged claw. In such instances the wound will bleed profusely, but do not be alarmed, as clotting occurs quite readily if the damage is not too severe; only if the claw is completely broken will it continue to bleed for any appreciable length of time.

Applying a cold solution of potassium aluminum sulphate with the aid of a cotton-tipped applicator will usually prove effective.

Overgrown claws are a common occurrence among Conures kept in captivity and are often the cause of an individual becoming caught up in wire-netting or branches and injuring itself. You can ask a qualified veterinary

surgeon to clip them if you are unsure of how to go about the task, but it is quite simple to do it yourself. All you need is a sharp pair of nail clippers rather than scissors. Restrain the bird by wrapping it loosely in a thick hand towel, from which only the legs and feet should be allowed to protrude. In species with pale-colored claws the blood supply can be seen quite clearly as a thin red streak, usually terminating at least ¼-inch (0.6 cm) from the tip.

Clip away the tip of each claw, allowing a generous margin to prevent bleeding. Pet birds are more likely to suffer from overgrown toenails than those which are kept outdoors and afforded plenty of natural exercise.

It is possible to purchase tubular sandsheets designed to fit over the dowelling perches, with the aim of keeping the claws in trim by

Egg-bound Orange-flanked Parakeet (*Brotogeris pyrrhopterus*) being held over steam. Never hold the bird less than eight inches away from the source of the steam.

"Conures often form strong pair bonds, and the recovery of the ailing half of a partnership may be greatly speeded if it can remain within sight and sound of its mate, provided that it is not suffering from any infectious disease."

Red-masked Conure (*Aratinga erythrogenys*) getting its beak trimmed. This procedure is best left to a professional the first few times.

virtue of constant filing action. In reality the beak action of your pet Conure is more likely to destroy these sandsheets long before they have had a chance to have any beneficial effect on the bird's pedicure.

Pet birds are also more inclined to need their beak trimmed from time to time. The upper mandible is the one most likely to become elongated, preventing the Conure from being able to feed properly. It too can be trimmed using a sharp pair of nail clippers. Unfortunately, when the bill has been clipped once, it tends to grow all the faster.

Although parasitic worms are more likely to be a problem among members of the Australian Parakeet

The Patagonian Conure (*Cyanoliseus patagonus*) prefers a small tree trunk to a nest box. Be sure, however, that such a trunk is parasite-free before placing it with the birds.

family, Conures may be subjected to these pests from time to time. Despite having been discovered as a pestilence affecting parrots as recently as the 1950s, the roundworm (*Ascaridia columbae*) is the most common type of parasitic worm likely to be found among Conures. It is quite large, measuring up to 1½ inches (4 cm) when adult and appears among the droppings as a dirty-white colored stringlike filament with tapered ends.

Female worms can lay up to 1000 eggs a day, and once an outbreak occurs the spread is likely to be very rapid. As Conures will spend a fair amount of time on the ground, they are particularly susceptible to contagion. In warm weather a whole collection of birds will soon

Canary-winged Parakeet (*Brotogeris versicolorus chiriri*). The lifespan of well-cared for brotogerids and Conures can often reach 15 years or more.

Thick-billed Parakeet (*Rhynchopsitta pachyrhyncha*), a close relative of the true Conures. Many experts believe that parrots kept in outdoor aviaries are hardier and more resistant to disease than indoor birds.

"As far as worms are concerned, prevention is better than cure."

become infected. As far as worms are concerned, prevention is better than cure. A semi-annual routine dosing with a suitable medicament is recommended, but one should refrain from offering any form of treatment during the breeding season, when the birds may be unduly stressed by the necessary handling involved.

One method of treatment is by means of a crop-tube attached to a hypodermic syringe, squirting the solution directly into the crop. Offering a suitable substance in the drinking water has the advantage that it does not necessitate capturing the birds, but then one can never be certain as to whether or not the correct dosage has been imbibed.

Unfortunately, no manufacturer has yet perfected an entirely tasteless preparation to be used in treatment. Best of those currently available is mebendazole, which has only a very slight taste when dissolved in water. When treating Conures it should be diluted in nine parts of water, and 1 ml of the diluted solution should be given per bird for three or four consecutive days. It will be taken less reluctantly if prepared fresh every day, and it is a good idea to deprive your birds of their water supply for a few hours beforehand, so that they will immediately need to drink and will imbibe a reasonable quantity before the taste begins to precipitate.

Stress is a factor affecting the well-being of many parrotlike birds, and although it is more likely to manifest itself in conditions such as severe feather plucking in the larger Macaws, Amazons and African Greys, it can still cause problems in the highly intelligent members of the Conure tribe. Feather plucking is a condition which has never been fully understood but, in all probability, boredom is one of the main contributory factors.

A poor diet consisting of nothing other than seed may be responsible in certain cases. Lack of bathing facilities and the absence of regular spraying may cause some individuals to start plucking themselves. Boredom and the frustrated desire to reproduce have all been cited as among the root causes of this distressing problem.

Stress may also be caused by over-crowding; an individual which is constantly being bullied cannot be expected to live a happy existence. It can be brought on by a move to new quarters or any other change in the bird's normal routine. One good reason for hand-rearing is that hand-fed Conures fear very little and are therefore less inclined to suffer stress-related symptoms.

Orange-flanked Parakeet (*Brotogeris pyrrhopterus*). Note the bright, healthy-looking plumage on this bird.

Brown-throated Conure (*Aratinga pertinax*). Members of this species are often seen living in towns and villages; they don't fear humans greatly and are therefore usually not known to become ill because of stress.

"A Conure suffering from any form of eye disease should be separated from its companions immediately, in case the condition is contagious."

A Conure suffering from any form of eye disease should be separated from its companions immediately, in case the condition is contagious. Irritation will cause the bird to rub its eyes on the perch and, therefore, thorough washing and immersion of the perch in disinfectant is advised to prevent the possible spread of disease.

Aureomycin is one of the most effective preparations in treating any type of infectious eye disease. A deficiency of vitamin A can result in the development of certain inflammatory eye conditions. An elderly Conure may develop cataracts and, unfortunately, there is no cure for these.

The development of antibiotics specially formulated for use by the bird-keeper has resulted in tremendous advancement in the treatment of avian illnesses, but they must be used with care. Their overuse can be extremely dangerous, as all manner of bacteria

if it presses on the bird's wind-pipe.

One of the most common problems associated with the female Conure is that of egg-binding—the inability of the egg to pass through the oviduct. An egg-bound female will desert her nest and sit dejectedly on the perch, eyes partially closed and wings drooping. Remedial action must be immediate if the bird is to make a recovery. Remove the affected individual to a hospital cage, where the temperature should be approximately 90°F (32°C), or place an infra-red lamp beside the cage, having first transferred the cock bird to alternative quarters.

In many instances the supply of heat will help to relax the tense muscles surrounding the oviduct and the egg will be laid in the normal manner, although this may not occur until the following day. Often the egg produced will be of the soft-shelled variety and will serve no use for incubation.

Egg-binding most commonly occurs during cold weather and the fact that most Conures have access to nesting facilities throughout the year, on account of their need for a secluded and well-protected roost, means that occasional out-of-season breeding attempts are unavoidable. However, given the right climatic conditions, the right nest-box and a suitable diet on which to raise their young, there is no reason why many species should not be successful in their attempts.

"One of the most common problems associated with the female Conure is that of egg-binding—the inability of the egg to pass through the oviduct."

(good and bad) are then killed, leaving the bird with virtually no resistance to disease whatsoever. Sadly, some importers of the more common Conure species treat their drinking water with antibiotics as a matter of course, but such practices are to be deplored.

The provision of iodine nibbles will rectify any deficiency of iodine, the lack of which can be responsible for the enlargement of the thyroid gland, which can result in respiratory problems

Young Dusky-headed Conures, *Aratinga weddellii*. This species is reputed to be a relatively quiet conure, and not strongly inclined to gnaw.

Breeding

Conures are becoming increasingly restricted in terms of the numbers of imported stocks being brought into Europe and the USA on account of the growing, albeit belated awareness of various South American governments that local flora and fauna must be preserved.

It is for this reason, and the consequent extra cost of acquiring these birds, that many owners are making greater attempts than ever before to reproduce from the dwindling numbers of adult breeding pairs being imported.

Captive-bred specimens are generally far more ready to go to nest than imported stocks, and nowadays many species are being bred to second and third generations and beyond. Only by encouraging these birds to breed under captive conditions can their future existence outside their countries of origin be assured. With the ever-increasing destruction of natural habitat, the continued survival of many species may rest entirely in the hands of the aviculturist.

In the past, hundreds of thousands of Conures would be exported on an annual basis and their prices were such that few owners ever bothered to give them the opportunity to breed. It is for this reason, coupled with the fact that they offer a somewhat greater challenge than the ever-prolific Australian Parakeets, that methods of Conure breeding in captivity are still relatively in their infancy.

It is heartening that this trend is gradually being reversed and the recent

Orange-flanked Parakeet (*Brotogeris pyrrhopterus*) demonstrating its aggressive breeding season behavior.

"Nansun" Conure female, a hybrid of the Nanday Conure (*Nandayus nenday*) and the Sun Conure (*Aratinga solstitialis*). In general, hybridization is not recommended.

development of surgical sexing methods is more than partly responsible for this change of fortunes. Unfortunately, none of the Conure species can be sexually identified by means of physical appearance or behavioral characteristics. Skilled veterinary surgeons have removed the element of doubt and, in many cases, saved aviculturists years of trial and error with two birds of the same sex.

The *Aratingas* are generally far less inquisitive in nature when compared with the extremely curious *Pyrrhuras*; they therefore tend to take much longer to get around to investigating possible nesting sites. *Aratinga* Conures will produce an average clutch of four eggs, while the *Pyrrhuras* frequently lay up to double that number.

In temperate climates Conures are invariably single-brooded in view of the comparatively lengthy incubation (averaging 26 days) compared with the three-week stint undertaken by the Australian Parakeets and the even longer period of time which their youngsters spend in the nest (seven or eight weeks). As it normally takes at least two weeks for the newly fledged brood to become independent, the breeding cycle for most Conures extends for approximately three months.

Of all the more commonly imported species, the Red-bellied can be regarded as perhaps the most prolific, but probably only on account of the free availability which it has enjoyed for many years. If other *Pyrrhura* species had been imported on such a regular basis over the past few decades, there is no reason why they should not have been able to emulate its reproductive success.

Given a choice between a natural hollowed-out log and a standard nest-box, the former would be the obvious choice of most pairs. Be prepared to offer a wide choice of nesting facilities, especially when setting up new breeding pairs.

Fitting a lining of wire-mesh or tin-plate may be advisable for the more destructive members of the Conure family. Although not as damaging in their habits as the larger South American species, some pairs are certainly capable of ravaging

the inside of the nest-box to the extent that both eggs and chicks come crashing to the floor. It therefore pays to adopt some form of preventive measure to reduce the incidence of such tragedies.

Some hens will tolerate very little in the way of nest-lining

Female Sun Conure (*Aratinga solstitialis*) incubating an egg.

The egg is now a 39-day-old chick.

Note how much neater the plumage is on the chick, now 43 days old.

Squawking 50-day-old Sun Conure. Fledging in most *Aratinga* species occurs right about this time.

Above: A pair of Sun Conure (*Aratinga solstitialis*) eggs. *Center:* Blue-crowned Conure (*Aratinga acuticaudata*). In the wild this species nests in a hollow tree.

A pair of Orange-flanked Parakeets (*Brotogeris pyrrhopterus*) inspecting their nest box. Brotogerids often chew on the entrance until they get it just right.

material, preferring to incubate their eggs on the bare wooden base of the nest-box. Others will appreciate the provision of a 2–3 inch (5–8 cm) layer of leaf mold, peat and rotting wood chippings, which they will chew up to their satisfaction.

Never use sawdust and/or wood shavings to line the nest-box, as this type of material tends to become extremely dry and can cause the eggs to be dead-in-shell. In this respect it may be advisable to

dampen the eggs slightly a few days before they are due to hatch. Make sure that the parents have access to regular bathing facilities, as they will then transfer a certain amount of moisture to the eggs during the brooding process.

Wait until the nest is temporarily unoccupied and, using a fine mist sprayer, lightly douse the clutch. Never attempt to do so while

incubation is taking place, even if the sitting bird is prepared to move slightly to one side when you open the inspection door.

If the nest-box is situated in the shelter close to the feeding hatch, occasional inspection of nesting operations may be that much easier. Most Conures will adopt a nest-box located undercover if they have any choice in the matter, as they feel more secure in a dimly lit environment. Unfortunately, it is more difficult to maintain the humidity level in a nest-box which is not subjected to the odd downpour of rain.

A standard-sized Cockatiel nest-box will suffice for all but the very largest members of the Conure family. Do not worry if the nest-box selected by any particular pair appears a little on the small side, as

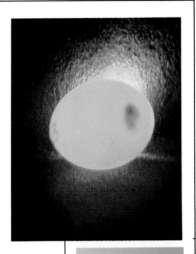

may be totally ignored by the pair in question. Ideally the entrance should be situated away from direct sunlight and other disturbances, such as the nightly penetration of car headlights or a neighbor's busy kitchen.

After about a week of incubation (not necessarily seven days after the laying of the first egg), you can check for signs of fertility. Once you have gained the experience of handling a number of fertile and infertile eggs, you will soon learn to spot the difference. Those which contain a chick take on a dullish gray-white appearance while the color of infertile

Above left: This clear egg may be infertile or it may be a newly laid egg that hasn't begun to develop. *Above right:* An egg that started to develop, but the embryo subsequently died. *Center:* Three-week-old Red-masked Conure (*Aratinga erythrogenys*). *Below left:* Week-old well-developing embryo. *Below right:* Almost fully developed chick.

most Conures will choose the smallest receptacle available to them—again probably because they feel more secure within its more restricted confines.

The entrance hole should be only just large enough for the pair to be able to squeeze through. If it is made too large, its potential as the threshold to their first home

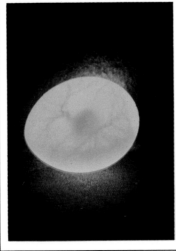

Above: **Nine-day-old Red-masked Conure chick beside a Red-masked egg. Note how much the youngster has grown in such a short time.** *Below:* **Candling eggs with the help of a Probe-light. When the lightbulb in the end of the handle is placed against the egg, the embryo inside can be seen. The long handle on this device allows eggs to be candled without being removed from the nest.**

eggs remains pinkish-white throughout the incubation period. Holding eggs up to the light will help to ascertain their viability, but as some pairs may object to their eggs being handled in this manner, it may pay to invest in a "Probe-lite."

With this simple piece of equipment one can candle eggs and check for fertility without even touching them and with no need to remove them from the nest. Simply extend the long, flexible wire so that it touches against each egg in turn with the attached tiny bright light; thus one can instantly distinguish between those eggs which stand a good chance of hatching and those which have no hope of doing so. Being battery powered, it is quite convenient to operate this ingenious piece of gadgetry in outside aviaries. It is also possible to use it to gently move newly hatched chicks to check whether they are being fed by their parents.

Most Conure hens rely upon their mate to bring food to the nest for the sustenance of their offspring. It is also the hen who alone carries out the task of incubation, although the male may sit beside her in the nest for quite long periods.

Above: Cork is a very popular nest lining with many Conures. *Center:* It is a good idea to keep tabs on the weight of young chicks. *Below:* Incubators with automatic turners are available, but most breeders still prefer to turn the eggs by hand.

One way to stimulate reluctant breeding pairs may be to furnish their nest-box with pieces of cork panelling. Generally sold in 1 ft (31 cm) squares for flooring purposes, the trick is to cut them into small segments and stick them around the internal walls of the nest-box in a haphazard fashion. Use a non-toxic glue for this purpose. Stick a whole tile onto the bottom of the nesting receptacle and cover

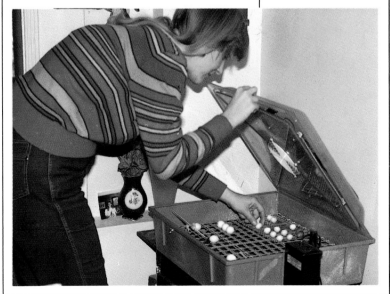

Five-week-old Canary-winged Parakeet (*Brotogeris versicolorus chiriri*). Note the well-developed wings as contrasted with the downy body.

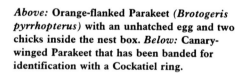

Above: Orange-flanked Parakeet (*Brotogeris pyrrhopterus*) with an unhatched egg and two chicks inside the nest box. *Below:* Canary-winged Parakeet that has been banded for identification with a Cockatiel ring.

it with a layer of peat.

A number of breeders have tried this method with success. Inexplicably, the presence of the cork seems to act as a stimulus where certain formerly unprolific pairs are concerned. The accessible pieces of the cork will soon be chewed apart and a clutch of eggs will often appear soon afterwards.

Since not all Conures are the most reliable parents, it may be necessary to resort to the use of foster parents. The Red-bellied species has often been employed for this purpose, although others may prove equally adaptable. The younger the chicks offered for fostering, the higher are their chances of being accepted.

Unfortunately, there may not always be a suitable pair available for carrying out fostering duties, as the surrogate parents must have chicks of their own at a roughly equivalent age, if one is to have any chance of success. In such instances it may be necessary to resort to hand-rearing.

Above: Nine-week-old Blue-crowned Conures *(Aratinga acuticaudata)* in a cage set aside for weaning. The wire flooring helps to keep these youngsters clean. *Below left:* Tovi and Cobalt-winged Parakeets *(Brotogeris jugularis* and *Brotogeris cyanoptera)* that have not yet been weaned. *Below right:* Five-week-old Tovi Parakeet, another unweaned youngster.

Seven-week-old
hand-reared
Cobalt-winged
Parakeet
(*Brotogeris
cyanoptera*).

Hand-rearing

Conures are excellent subjects for hand-rearing, and a youngster which has been handled from a very early age will make an extremely trusting and loving pet. Such birds are thus much sought after as pets and many breeders make a point of hand-rearing at least a percentage of the year's progeny with this demand in mind.

In certain circumstances, pulling chicks from the nest in this way may persuade the parents to go on to produce a second round, thus doubling up on their breeding potential. At other times removing chicks from the nest may be a matter of life and death if their parents have deserted them or are simply not feeding them correctly. Many lives have been saved by the willingness of the owner to become a surrogate parent.

It is true to state that the younger the chicks are drawn from the nest, the more problems one is likely to experience in persuading them to accept an artificial diet, one which does not contain all the proper microflora passed on by the parents as an aid to digestion, thus helping the chicks to develop and grow properly. All Conure chicks will receive a better start in life if they can remain with their parents or foster parents for as long a period as possible—at least for the first few days after hatching.

Before you attempt the task, you should be aware that you are undertaking a time-consuming and laborious chore which will last for up to ten weeks, when the youngster finally attains independence. If you are attempting to hand-

"Conures are excellent for hand-rearing, and a youngster which has been handled from a very early age will make an extremely trusting and loving pet."

It is especially important to ensure that the cages housing young chicks are clean and very hygienic.

Six-week-old Tovi Parakeet (*Brotogeris jugularis*) being hand-fed. The temperature of the food must be just right.

It is also imperative that the chicks be kept in warm quarters. This set-up utilizes an electric heating pad under a five-gallon aquarium.

rear a chick which is under three days old, it will require hourly feeding throughout the day, commencing at first light. Older chicks need sustenance every two to four hours.

If you are attempting your first effort at hand-rearing, it is advisable to start off with a partly fledged youngster, which will not present so many problems, but few who are forced to take on the task initially have any choice in

the age and species of their first charge.

A purpose-built brooder is not essential from the outset, as any thermostatically controlled hospital cage or still-air incubator will suffice. In any case a brooder is simply a small wooden box, fitted with a glass top and heated by means of two 60–watt electric light bulbs attached to a thermostat to control the degree of heat (a cheap and perfectly adequate thermostat can be purchased from most aquarist shops). The bulbs must be positioned in such a way that the chicks are never allowed to come into direct contact with them to prevent the possibility of scalding.

In the event of such an accident occurring, if the burn is not too severe, spray it with cold water. Do not apply any form of ointment. In the case of a more serious wound, an anti-inflammatory spray should be applied. Unfortunately, if very young

Tovi Parakeet being fed with an eyedropper. The younger the chick being hand-fed, the more often the meals must be given.

chicks suffer a burn like this, it is likely that the shock alone will kill them. Therefore, prevention really is the answer, rather than trying to effect a cure.

As an emergency measure an ordinary angle-poise lamp can be suspended over a small box, with the beam directed towards the chick. Never rely upon a source of heat from beneath the floor of the box as there is a risk of overheating.

If you have a number of chicks being hand-reared at the same time, it is a good idea to place them individually in separate small containers within the brooder. Empty margarine tubs of different sizes are ideal for this purpose.

Conure chicks are quite vociferous in expressing their demands even at a very early age, and if you have chicks of different stages of development being hand-reared (and if possible), it is advisable to place them in individual brooders in separate rooms in the house. This is because older chicks

which require only two- to four-hourly feedings will soon become aroused by the sounds of younger offspring being fed more often and will clamorously demand to be fed at the same time.

For very young chicks the brooder should initially be pre-set at 99°F (37°C)—the same temperature as employed for hatching purposes. Once they are a few days old the temperature can be dropped to 95°F (35°C) and

Young brotogerid strolling by an incubator full of eggs. This contraption has a fan that controls temperature and humidity.

Golden-crowned Conure (*Aratinga aurea*) and a Senegal Parrot (*Poicephalus senegalus*) inside an incubating tank.

Four-week-old Nanday Conure (*Nandayus nenday*).

after a week or so, it can be lowered to 90⁰F (32°C). These figures serve only as a guideline; you should carefully monitor the temperature of the brooder at all times and adjust it accordingly if the chicks appear to be uncomfortable at any time. Individuals vary a great deal, and what will serve well for one chick may not necessarily suit another youngster—even one of the same species.

If several small chicks are being cared for together in a brooder, they will cluster together; if a group is widely spaced, this is an obvious sign that they are too hot. Restlessness and panting with the beak open are additional signs that the temperature should be lowered. If a chick seems lethargic and is slow to digest its food, then it may be taken for granted that it is suffering the effects of cold.

Remember that chicks of the larger Conure species can maintain a higher level of body temperature than the offspring of smaller species. A group of chicks will not require the same intensity of heat that will be needed by a youngster being hand-reared on its own. If there is a degree of variation in the ages of chicks being reared in a brooder together, the correct temperature will be dictated by the requirements of the youngest.

Use a lining of tissue paper in the base of the brooder or place a single tissue in the bottom of a margarine tub. In this way the young Conure will be better able to gain a grip and its feet will not be forced to slide about on a slippery surface. It is also a good idea to pick up a chick using a piece of tissue, especially if one's hands are likely to be cold at the time. Alternatively, rinse them under warm water before handling.

A damp paper towel rather than tissue paper should be used to wipe off any excess food which may be spilled during the feeding process. Pay careful attention to the area around the mouth to prevent the incidence of infection. Use a cotton-tipped applicator to get right inside the mouth.

As with most South American parrots, in both *Aratinga* and *Pyrrhura* Conure chicks the ear opening remains closed for up to a month after hatching. Those who have kept Cockatiels or Australian Parakeets might regard this as an abnormality, but it is certainly no cause for concern.

Recipes for a suitable hand-rearing diet are as numerous as those for homemade fruitcake. If you have a tried

and tested formula, then the best advice is to stick to it. Some breeders go to quite unnecessary lengths to prepare their own specially formulated rearing foods, but the best advice for those who are inexperienced at hand-rearing is to purchase proprietary baby foods.

A whole variety of excellent cereal preparations are marketed for feeding human babies and these are just as suitable to provide a complete diet for young Conures. For the first few days canned baby foods can be given (bone and beef broth with vegetables and fruit dessert are ideal). With water added, the two can be given in equal proportions, making sure that both are of the same consistency (as runny as milk) when feeding very young chicks and increasing the solidity of the

"Recipes for a suitable hand-rearing diet are as numerous as those for homemade fruitcake."

Nanday Conure, 12 days old, being hand-fed with an eyedropper. Note the pinpoint where the feathers are coming in.

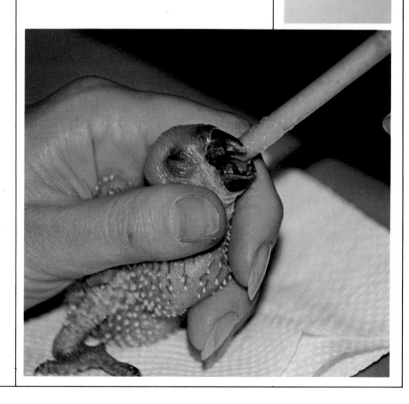

Above and below: Cobalt-winged Parakeet (*Brotogeris cyanoptera*) at 19 days (above) and 30 days (below).

providing a slightly poor quality diet rather than one which is over-rich.

As their feathers start to appear, the chicks can be introduced to small quantities of seed (ground sunflower kernels, for instance, which are available ready hulled from health food shops) and pureed vegetables. Again, increase the solidity gradually over a period of time.

If a chick proves difficult to feed, shaking its head and accepting very little at the stage when it is more or less fully feathered, then it is ready to wean—and thus begins the most irksome aspect of the hand-rearing process. Conures and other neo-tropical species are notoriously difficult in this respect, and much patience will be needed to persuade them to accept an adult diet.

Start off by offering soaked foods, such as sunflower seeds and millet sprays. A small amount of whole fruit can be incorporated into the diet at this stage; pear is ideal for this purpose. You will probably have to continue to offer seed in soaked form for some weeks. Weaning is essentially a gradual process, reducing the number of daily feedings until the chicks are being spoon-fed only once a day and finally not at all.

Conure chicks will accept the process of being spoon-fed from the earliest stage after being removed from the nest. It should never be necessary to use a syringe or an eye-dropper to feed a healthy chick. All one needs is an

food as the youngsters progress.

Remember that, again like human babies, Conure chicks cannot tolerate a diet which is too rich during the early stages of their development. It is better to err on the side of

ordinary teaspoon with the sides bent upward and inward. Offered food in this way, the chick can employ the normal pumping action which it requires to be able to obtain food from its parents. It is important that the spoon be warmed beforehand to the same temperature as the food being provided, otherwise the chick may simply refuse to eat. Warm both the food and

as soon as possible if breeding is the aim. On the other hand, if one wants a tame, confiding pet, then there is no better choice than a hand-reared youngster. Its trust in the human race as a whole will be implicit.

Above: Orange-flanked Parakeet (*Brotogeris pyrrhopterus*) at 6½ weeks. *Center:* Jandaya Conure (*Aratinga jandaya*) having a snack. *Below:* Orange-flanked Parakeet at nine weeks of age.

the utensil in a small saucepan; for very young chicks it should be fairly hot, gradually decreasing the temperature as they grow older.

It is wrong to assume that hand-reared Conures will never accept their own kind and make good parents themselves, although it is essential that they be reunited with their own kind

The Species

Conures and Parakeets—what is the difference? Essentially there isn't one, although the former term is generally applied only to the South American species and principally those of either the genus *Aratinga* or *Pyrrhura*. The genus *Nandayus* is represented by the popular Nanday Conure. In addition, members of the genus *Brotogeris* are commonly called Conures.

One specific distinction between the two largest genera is the amount of noise which they are likely to generate. *Aratingas* have a bad reputation for exercising their shrill, ear-piercing notes at every opportunity, while members of the *Pyrrhura* group are of a much quieter disposition.

The *Aratingas* range in size from 14 inches (36 cm) down to 7 inches (18 cm); they are invariably light green in color, with various color head markings—primarily red, orange, blue and brown. On the other hand, the *Pyrrhuras* are a much darker green, with scaled markings on the throat, nape and upper regions of the breast. Size does not vary so much between the various species, with a maximum length of 11 inches (28 cm) and a minimum of 8 inches (20 cm).

GENUS *ARATINGA*

The larger members of this group, such as the Queen of Bavaria's Conure, closely resemble the smaller Macaws, differing only insofar as they

Opposite: **A pair of Slender-billed Conures (*Enicognathus leptorhynchus*). These parrots are highly gregarious and very noisy.**

"One specific distinction between the two largest genera is the amount of noise they are likely to generate."

Petz's Conure (*Aratinga canicularis*) and Canary-winged Parakeet (*Brotogeris versicolorus chiriri*).

sport feathered lores and cheeks; the naked eyering is also a prominent feature. Typically, the predominantly light green coloration is sharply contrasted by the splash of color on the bird's head. Two exceptions are the Sun Conure and the aforementioned Queen of Bavaria's, which are the only members of this group which do not display mainly green coloring.

Apart from their raucous voices (again, the Queen of Bavaria's springs to mind as one of the worst culprits in this respect), most of the *Aratingas* are extremely destructive towards woodwork. It is these two factors which prevent many enthusiasts from recognizing their potential as pets. In fact, these birds are often highly intelligent and many will learn to mimic their owner's

Above: Blue-crowned Conure (*Aratinga acuticaudata*). Wild members of this species will often allow humans to get quite close. *Right:* Golden-capped Conure (*Aratinga auricapilla*). *Opposite:* Artist's rendering of various *Aratinga* Conures.

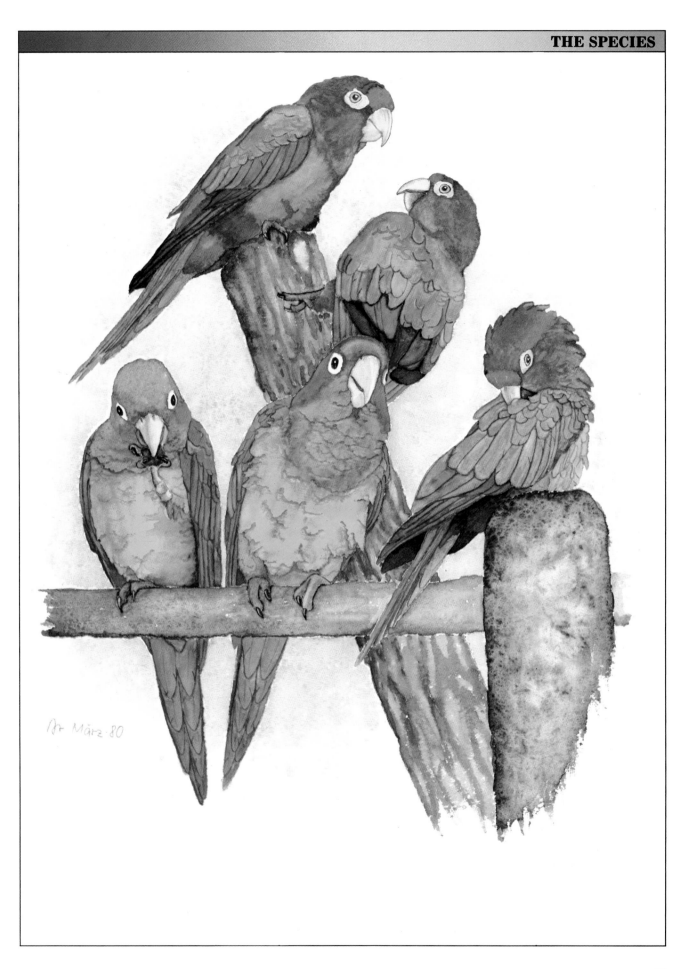

female, but this cannot be relied upon as a means of distinction).

Although certain members of the *Pyrrhura* group have been successfully bred on the colony system from time to time, this method cannot be recommended with the larger *Aratingas*, unless the accommodation provided is extremely large, enabling each pair to establish its own

Finsch's Conure (*Aratinga finschi*). When flying in a flock, these birds move almost in unison.

voice if they are obtained at a sufficiently early age. In terms of behavior, they are lively and entertaining.

One problem for the would-be breeder is that the sexes appear to be identical (some fanciers believe that there is a difference in head size and shape between male and

Right: Olive-throated Conure (*Aratinga nana*). In the wild this species often damages local corn crops.
Far right: Mitred Conure (*Aratinga mitrata*).

A pair of Brown-throated Conures (*Aratinga pertinax*). These birds are especially noisy when in flight.

Far left: The Green Conure (*Aratinga holochlora*) has been known to roost in old woodpecker holes. *Left:* Adult male Red-fronted Conure (*Aratinga wagleri*).

small area of territory. Clutch sizes range from two to six eggs and incubation is undertaken by the female alone, generally for a period of 26 days. Youngsters will remain in the nest for up to seven or eight weeks and it is usually another 14 days before they become fully independent.

Golden-crowned Conure (*Aratinga aurea*). Members of this species may be able to learn a few words.

Golden-crowned Conure (*Aratinga aurea*)

Otherwise known as the Peach-fronted Conure (especially in the USA), this 10-inch (25 cm) species is one of the most popular and commonly imported members of its genus. It is also reasonably free-breeding. Occasionally it is confused with the even more favored and closely related Petz's Conure, to which it bears a distinct resemblance.

Its basic coloration is dark green above, shading to lighter green on the underparts. This somewhat austere color scheme is relieved by the bright orange feathers of the forehead and upper regions of the crown. A similarly colored ring of feathers surrounds the eyes. Behind the crown is an area of blue; the cheeks and throat are olive.

The tail is green above tipped with blue, merging into an olive shade underneath, tinges of which extend to the lower part of the breast. Principally a bluish shade, the primaries are tipped with black. The iris is brown and the bill is black.

Youngsters differ from adults in having a horn-colored beak and a pale gray iris; the areas of blue and orange on the head are less extensive and they also lack the ring of orange feathers surrounding the eye. Immature birds therefore bear an even greater resemblance to Petz's Conure.

In their natural range, these birds are extremely widespread, being found throughout Brazil, with the exception of certain coastal regions and the extreme southeastern part of the country. They are also found in northern Paraguay, northwestern parts of Argentina and eastern Bolivia. They favor semi-open countryside.

In the USA the Golden-crowned has never been as commonly available as Petz's Conure, although the situation is reversed as far as European enthusiasts are concerned. Hybrids between the two species have been produced from time to time (keep in mind, however, that it is not advisable to deliberately set out to produce youngsters of mixed parentage).

Captive breeding successes were rarely recorded until a few years ago, but nowadays this species is being

reproduced quite regularly in the USA and more occasionally with European collections. The first recorded breeding occurred over 100 years ago.

Although neither as destructive nor as vociferous as other members of the genus, the Golden-crowned is quite capable of damaging unprotected woodwork and its voice can be ear-piercingly shrill at times.

Nesting may occur quite early in the year—late April or early May—and the average clutch size is three or four eggs. Not the most fastidious of feeders, the Golden-crowned should prove quite simple to cater to, requiring few extras for the successful rearing of its offspring.

Greenfood, however, is not a popular item of the diet, although individuals will avidly consume all manner of fruit.

Apart from Petz's, this species has hybridized with both Cactus (*A. cactorum*) and Jandaya Conures. A subspecies known as the Greater Golden-crowned Conure (*A.a. major*) exists and differs from the nominate form in being slightly larger, as its name would suggest. It is nowhere near as widespread in its natural habitat, being found only in parts of Paraguay.

As a pet the Golden-crowned Conure is perhaps not the most outstanding candidate for choice, mainly on account of its harsh vocalizations. Nevertheless, if taken young, there is no reason why an individual might not prove its worth.

Petz's Conure
(*Aratinga canicularis*)

Otherwise known as the Orange-flanked or Halfmoon Conure—the latter term more often applied by American enthusiasts—this is the pet Conure par excellence. Especially in the USA, it is the species which has been responsible for introducing many enthusiasts to the hobby. Commonly hand-reared, it is remarkable for the readiness with which it will accept its owner.

As previously mentioned,

this species is often confused with the Golden-crowned, but identification is quite simple if one remembers that the bill is basically horn colored rather than black. However, it is worth remembering that youngsters of the Golden-crowned also have the horn-colored bill, although in their case the lower mandible will

blue, as are the secondaries which are etched with a bordering edge of green; the wings are otherwise predominantly green. There is an area of bare yellow skin surrounding the eye, and in this respect Petz's Conure again differs from the Golden-crowned in which these regions are covered with

not be partly black as is the case with both adult and young Petz's Conures.

As with the Golden-crowned, the basic coloration is green; being of a slightly yellowish shade on the underparts and underwing and tail coverts. Part of the crown and the forehead is orange and towards the nape the color is

encircling orange feathers. Length is 9½ inches (24 cm). Youngsters display only a little orange on the forehead and the iris is brown instead of yellow.

Petz's Conure is extremely common throughout much of its range and in many areas it is the most frequently encountered member of the

"Apart from its nesting habits, the Petz's Conure is strictly arboreal and will seldom descend to the ground even when kept in an aviary."

parrot family. It inhabits the western side of Central America as far south as western Costa Rica.

In the wild, nesting sites are usually within occupied termite mounds, with both male and female taking part in the excavation work. Usually they form an entrance hole close to the base of the mound, tunnelling upwards for a further 12–18 inches (31–46 cm), before channelling inward to form the nesting chamber within the softer interior material.

On completion (normally after about a week), the nesting chamber will measure approximately 6–9 inches (18–23 cm) in diameter and will be left unoccupied for a further seven days, presumably to enable the termites to make good any necessary repairs to the main structure of the mound.

Apart from its nesting habits, the Petz's Conure is strictly arboreal and will seldom descend to the ground even when kept in an aviary.

No breeding records exist in the UK and successes have been scarce throughout Europe. However, in the USA it is a completely different story and pairs have even been known to breed in a

Petz's Conure (*Aratinga canicularis*) having its breakfast.

In the wild, Petz's Conures dig tunnels for nests in termite mounds; quite often the male does most of this work.

small cage with a suitable nest-box attached to the outside. Throughout the late 1970s and early 1980s quite large numbers of captive-bred youngsters have been produced and many have been hand-reared, often especially for the pet trade.

Its high standing as a pet is perhaps somewhat surprising in view of the fact that its voice is no less raucous than that of any other member of the *Aratinga* family. Young birds are utterly fearless; many will learn to talk and some can even be persuaded to perform a few tricks for the entertainment of their owner.

"Young birds are utterly fearless; many will learn to talk and some can even be persuaded to perform a few tricks for the entertainment of their owner."

part of the ear coverts, the head is entirely red and also a few scattered red feathers are found on the bird's throat. Red is also apparent on the shoulders, underwing coverts and thighs.

The underside of the tail is a yellowish shade of green. The beak is yellowish-white. Length is approximately 13 inches (33 cm). Youngsters are easily distinguished, having no red on the head.

In the wild state this species inhabits northwestern Peru and southwestern parts of Ecuador, where it is to be found more generally in the arid tropical zones. Within its range it is fairly common.

Unfortunately, examples are only occasionally imported both into Europe and the USA, although they have been known to aviculture for the better part of the last century. Many regard this species as among the prettiest of the Conures and their only

Above and right: Red-masked Conure (*Aratinga erythrogenys*). Members of this species often roost in rock crevices.

Red-masked Conure (*Aratinga erythrogenys*)

Equally well-known as the Red-headed Conure, adults are extremely handsome, bearing a larger amount of coloring on the head than any other member of the group.

With the exception of the hind part of the cheeks and

drawback is once again their piercingly shrill voices.

Breeding records are fairly scant, although the species has been known to reproduce both in Great Britain and in the USA. Four eggs would seem to be the average clutch size.

With a little effort, youngsters taken young from the nest can become quite good talkers, and individuals have been reported as learning to mimic sounds such as those of a cackling hen. It may even be possible to teach one to return to its cage after a period of freedom in the room.

Queen of Bavaria's Conure (*Aratinga guarouba*)

Occasionally known as the Golden Conure, this large 14-inch (36 cm) species seemingly bears a closer relationship to the Macaw family with its typical naked eyerings. It is invariably regarded as the most desirable member of its genus and is much sought after by aviculturists. It is not a suitable subject for the totally inexperienced.

It is characterized by the light horn-colored beak, which appears massive in comparison with the remainder of the bird's predominantly golden-yellow

"Occasionally known as the Golden Conure, this . . . species seemingly bears a closer relationship to the Macaw family with its typical naked eyerings."

Fanciers of the Queen of Bavaria's Conure (*Aratinga guarouba*) often call it the most intelligent member of its genus.

Queen of Bavaria's Conures (*Aratinga guarouba*) are highly sociable among themselves but usually do not tolerate birds of other species.

"Despite their seemingly cumbersome appearance, these birds [Queen of Bavaria's Conures] are extremely agile and a pair will play together for hours."

coloring, lending a completely top-heavy semblance. Only the green primary and secondary flight feathers provide any relief coloration. The tail is short and tapered and the iris is either brown or black.

Youngsters are extremely variable in terms of coloration; some may sport only a few scattered green feathers on the upperwing coverts and occasionally on the cheeks, while others may be either predominantly green or yellow. They are generally of a much slimmer build than their parents.

In its natural habitat it is found in northeastern parts of Brazil south of the Amazon river. In the wild their strident voices carry for great distances and, unfortunately, they are no less vocal in captivity. Until you have heard a Queen of Bavaria's Conure in full cry, it is

difficult to imagine just how ear-shatteringly loud these birds are.

In shape and size this species is so unlike any other member of the *Aratinga* tribe that it is hard to fathom how they could be related. Like Macaws, they are prone to feather plucking—probably a manifestation of boredom.

Despite their seemingly cumbersome appearance, these birds are extremely agile and a pair will play together for hours. It is essential to provide them with a selection of toys, with which they have the chance to become fully occupied; otherwise they will entertain themselves by extracting their own and each others' feathers. Cocks have been known to completely chew off the tail of their intended mate.

These birds display a high degree of intelligence and they have great personalities. Unfortunately, they have always remained expensive as demand invariably outstrips supply. Another problem is that newly imported individuals are inclined to be somewhat delicate, requiring careful acclimatization. Youngsters may be particularly tricky and will need heat for some time before they become established.

In the wild their natural habitat is being rapidly destroyed and, therefore, it is becoming increasingly important to establish captive-bred strains.

Like so many of the Conures, sexing is the first step toward successfully setting up a breeding pair. It is said that the cock's upper mandible is slightly larger than that of his mate, but this cannot be relied upon as a reliable method of sexual identification. Once one has established a true pair (now that surgical sexing is becoming so much more widely available, there really is no excuse for maintaining same-sex "pairs" together for any length of time), captive-breeding should not prove too difficult to encourage.

Queen of Bavaria's Conures will usually go to nest in captivity and have done so on numerous occasions both in Europe and in the USA. Unfortunately, they are extremely aggressive during the breeding period—perhaps more so than any other Conure.

Clutch size averages three eggs. Both parents will tend the offspring from the day they hatch out, and the chicks are quite noisy even when only a few days old. At the age of six weeks they will be almost completely feathered, but it will be another month before they are ready to leave the nest. Initially the chicks may prove reluctant to use their wings, preferring to clamber around their enclosure rather than flying. They will continue to demand to be fed by their parents for at least two weeks after fledging.

An adult pair will require a highly nutritious diet while they have chicks in the nest to be fed. Corn-on-the-cob will be particularly appreciated. Huge amounts of water will be imbibed during the rearing process. No records of hybridizing exist.

Youngsters are well in demand as pets, but it should be noted that they require far more attention than the average small Conure and the acquisition of even a single Queen of Bavaria's should be given a great deal of consideration.

Unfortunately, like Macaws, they may be regarded as something of a status symbol, in view of their size and spectacular appearance. By all means, buy a young Queen of Bavaria's Conure if you have previously gained some measure of experience with the smaller *Aratingas* and *Pyrrhuras* and you welcome a challenge. It also helps if you are a little hard of hearing!

"By all means buy a Queen of Bavaria's Conure if you have previously gained some measure of experience with the smaller Aratingas and Pyrrhuras and you welcome the challenge."

Queen of Bavaria's Conures must be kept in somewhat humid conditions, as low humidity is often cited as a cause of feather plucking.

Compared to members of other species, Jandaya Conures (*Aratinga jandaya*) are rather well-behaved during the breeding season.

Jandaya Conure
(*Aratinga jandaya*)

Otherwise referred to as the Yellow-headed Conure, the vocal notes of this species are no less attractive than other members of the *Aratinga* genus. It has enjoyed changing fortunes as an avicultural subject. At one time it was much more common and more freely available than the closely related Sun Conure, but nowadays it is regarded as far more of a rarity.

One of the more brightly colored members of the *Aratinga* family, it is predominantly bright buttercup yellow on the head, neck and upper regions of the breast, and this coloring merges into the rich red of the bird's underparts. The upper parts are mainly green, with the exception of the lower regions of the bird's back which are vermilion. A few red feathers are

The Jandaya Conure is sometimes classified as a subspecies of the Sun Conure (*Aratinga solstitialis*) and as a subspecies of the Golden-capped Conure (*Aratinga auricapilla*).

distinguishable on the olive-green thighs and, in turn, the red breast is interspersed by the occasional splash of olive-green.

Both the flight feathers and the tip of the tail are bright blue, with the undertail coverts bronze colored, merging into a blackish hue. The bill is black and the iris is a dirty brown. Length is 12 inches (31 cm).

In immature plumage, youngsters differ in sporting a generally paler coloration, particularly with regard to the areas of red, orange and yellow, where many of the feathers are bordered in

Jandaya Conures
have been
hybridized with
Nanday
Conures
(*Nandayus
nenday*) and with
several *Aratinga*
species.

green and sometimes there is
a complete replacement by
patches of green coloration.

Breeding successes have
been quite numerous. Clutch
size averages three or four
eggs and the incubation
period is 26 days. Unlike other
members of the genus,
Jandaya chicks are
comparatively quick to fledge,
usually remaining in the nest
for only eight weeks. Both
cock and hen will feed the
youngsters, although the task
of brooding will remain the
sole responsibility of the hen.

Hybridization has taken
place on several occasions,
with both the Sun and the

In the wild,
Jandaya males
often share
incubation with
the females.

White-eyed Conure (*Aratinga leucophthalmus*). Members of this species often vary greatly in size.

Adult female White-eyed Conure. Within this species, all incubating is done by the female.

Nanday Conure as a partner. In the case of the former coupling, the chicks can be extremely attractive.

As a subject for the would-be pet owner, the potential of this species has not been fully explored. Its vociferous nature may prove to be a drawback, but individuals can be highly inquisitive and amusing acrobats.

White-eyed Conure (*Aratinga leucophthalmus*)

At last, in this species we have one which is not confused by the conferring of a multiplicity of alternative names. One reason for this could be that it has never enjoyed quite the same level of popularity as the aforementioned species.

Very occasionally it may be referred to simply as the Green Conure, but as this

rather unimaginative term could be applied equally well to the vast majority of Conure species, its use implies inaccuracy and is not to be recommended.

As can be discerned from the foregoing remarks, this species is primarily green in overall coloration, with the exception of the underwing coverts and the carpal edges of the wings which are red, as are a few scattered feathers on the bird's head. The undertail coverts and greater underwing coverts are a rich, golden yellow and the flights are characterized by dusky colored tips.

There is an area of bare white skin surrounding the eye. The powerful-looking bill is flesh colored. Length is approximately 13½ inches (35 cm). In appearance this species closely resembles the rare Hispaniolan Conure (*A. chloroptera*), although the latter is slightly shorter in overall length.

Juveniles are not readily distinguishable, despite the fact that they have the yellow carpal edge and some of the underwing coverts remain green rather than red or golden-yellow.

In distribution, this species ranges over an immensely wide area, occupying most of the northern parts of South America, with the exception of the western coastal regions. Its habitat extends to Venezuela and eastern Colombia southward to the northern parts of Paraguay and Argentina. In view of its widespread distribution, it is surprising that it has never been more commonly imported.

The comparatively small numbers coming into captivity both within Europe and the USA no doubt account for the fact that breeding has seldom taken place in captivity. It was first bred in the USA in the early 1930s and in the UK as recently as 1975.

This is one species which could do well kept in a small colony, as in the wild it is often to be seen in small groups of up to half a dozen individuals. It is extremely strong on the wing and it is shy and quick to take flight when alarmed. As with all *Aratingas*, the voice is harsh and discordant.

In spite of the small number of occasions on which this species has gone to nest in captivity, it has been known to be double-brooded. Clutch size averages four eggs, but only two or three may be laid.

In addition to the bird's normal diet, quite large amounts of greenfood may be consumed while there are chicks in the nest. Youngsters are likely to be 10–11 weeks old before emerging from the nest.

As this species has never been imported in very large numbers, its potential as a pet subject has never been fully explored. Undoubtedly much would depend on the age at which youngsters are taken from the nest, and a hand-reared specimen would be far more likely to become tame and confiding.

Sun Conure
(Aratinga solstitialis)
With no other name to confuse matters, this species is commonly regarded as the most attractive representative of the entire Conure group. Without being too garish, it is certainly a bird of outstanding beauty and one which has won a great many converts to the pleasure of Conure keeping.

"This [White-eyed Conure] is one species which could do well kept in a small colony, as in the wild it is often to be seen in small groups of up to half a dozen individuals."

Sun Conure (*Aratinga solstitialis*). This species has more yellow than its relative— according to some experts— the Jandaya Conure, which is often classified as *Aratinga solstitialis jandaya*.

The Sun Conure (*Aratinga solstitialis*) that is raised as an only bird will form a strong attachment to its owner.

Sun Conures have been hybridized with Golden-crowned Conures (*Aratinga aurea*).

Closely resembling the Jandaya in size—12 inches (31 cm)—and shape, its plumage is somewhat variable, making the task of providing a definitive description quite impossible. By way of generalization, it is mainly a mixture of yellow and vermilion, resulting in a particularly fiery appearance. No illustration could possibly do justice to the highly unique blending of such a dazzling riot of coloring.

The bird's head and underparts are fiery orange. The wings are yellow, with the secondaries showing the barest evidence of green. The tail is olive-green, sometimes merging into blue at the tip and on the outer webs of the feathers. Blue is also the color of the primaries. The undertail coverts are green shading into yellow. The bill is completely black and there is an area of whitish colored skin surrounding the eye.

Juveniles are even more variable in terms of coloration than their peers, having less orange on the head and underparts, which are inclined to be yellow rather than orange. They also sport more green on the wings.

This species is found in the Guyanas and in northwestern parts of Brazil. It generally occurs in quite large flocks.

It has been known to aviculturists for over a century, but only recently has it appeared in many European collections. Since the early 1970s when this species began to be more freely available, captive stocks have proved extremely prolific and pairs have been known to regularly raise broods of four or more chicks.

An exception rather than the rule, if exportation of the Sun Conure were suddenly to completely cease, there is little doubt that the current level of the captive population could be maintained as a result of the numbers being bred in captivity.

Sun Conures are invariably attentive parents; youngsters emerge from the egg after a period of 26–27 days. Chicks have grayish-white colored down and take eight to ten weeks before fledging.

Over the past decade or so many youngsters have been adopted as pets and they usually prove quite engaging in their mannerisms and quickly learn to accept their owner. Again their voices belie their pleasant characters.

Sun Conures are among the most prolific members of the genus *Aratinga*.

"With an alternative name of Weddell's Conure . . . individuals [Dusky-headed Conures] have the virtue of being nowhere near as loud-mouthed as other representatives of the genus.

Dusky-headed Conures (Aratinga weddellii) are reminiscent of small Macaws due to their large white eyerings.

Dusky-headed Conure (*Aratinga weddellii*)

With an alternative name of Weddell's Conure, as denoted by the specific name afforded to this species, individuals have the virtue of being nowhere near as loud-mouthed as other representatives of the genus.

The plumage is predominantly green, merging into a more yellowish shade on the underparts. The head is grayish-blue, with most of the feathers being tipped with blue. The tail is similarly tipped with blue, as are both the primaries and secondaries.

The upper parts are olive-green. The throat and upper regions of the breast are tinged with blue and the lower regions of the breast, abdomen and underwing coverts are olive-green. An

area of white skin surrounds the eye; this is more extensive than in other members of the group which share this feature. The bill is black and the iris is a distinctive pale gray color. Length is approximately 11½ inches (30 cm).

In immature plumage youngsters still closely resemble their parents; the only differences in appearance are the dark-colored iris and the slightly smaller size.

The Dusky-headed Conure is the most commonly encountered member of its genus around the southeastern parts of Colombia. It is also found over a large area of the Amazon basin in Peru, Bolivia, Ecuador, and western Brazil. In spite of its relatively common state in its native lands, it is still fairly scarcely imported into Europe and the USA, although numbers coming on to the American market in recent years have increased quite dramatically. As a result, prices have fallen and it is now among the more inexpensive *Aratingas*. Apart from their quieter disposition, they can be recommended for their good behavior in not chewing every piece of woodwork in sight.

None were known to have gone to nest successfully in captivity until the late 1970s, although several pairs have lately proved their reproductive ability. In most cases they have readily adapted to a typical Cockatiel nest-box, filled to a depth of

2–4 inches (5–10 cm) with suitable nesting material. Some pairs will eject this in no time at all, preferring to lay their eggs on the bare floor, although others enjoy their creature comforts far more. As always, pairs are highly individualistic.

Three eggs form the average clutch, although as many as seven have been produced. Incubation takes approximately 25 days. Dusky-headed Conures invariably make excellent parents and pairs have been used to foster the chicks of other less reliable species.

If the chicks are removed from the nest at an early age for hand-rearing they will make extremely affectionate pets and will often learn to mimic the voice of their keeper. Although not as colorful as other *Aratingas*, what they lack in terms of coloration they make up for by means of their lively personalities and engaging habits.

Three-month-old Dusky-headed Conure. Note how its beak has not turned completely black.

Artist's rendering of various brotogerids. *Top left:* Cobalt-winged Parakeet (*Brotogeris cyanoptera*). *Top right:* Tuipara Parakeet (*Brotogeris chrysopterus tuipara*), a subspecies of the Golden-winged Parakeet (*Brotogeris chrysopterus*). *Bottom left:* Canary-winged Parakeet (*Brotogeris versicolorus chiriri*). *Bottom right:* Tui Parakeet (*Brotogeris sanctithomae*).

GENUS *BROTOGERIS*

One question which is sometimes asked is what is the difference between a Conure and a Parakeet. Technically speaking, there is none. Conures are simply those Parakeets hailing from Central and South America. Although the term is never applied to Australian, African and Asiatic species, it is frequently conferred upon the attractive little group of *Brotogeris* Parakeets, which also find their home in South America.

All members of this group are small, measuring no more than 9 inches (23 cm) in total length, and they are mainly light green in coloration, with varying amounts of color

(primarily blue and yellow) on the forehead, crown, chin, and primaries and, in one instance, on the underwing coverts.

They have a solidly built appearance and a gradated tail. In overall dimensions they are similar to Lovebirds, but they are of a more slender, less dumpy build. The beak is of a shape similar to that of an Amazon parrot, with the upper mandible deeply hooked. A naked eyering is a characteristic of all members of the *Brotogeris* group. Sexes are alike and youngsters closely resemble adults.

In their native lands many species are overly abundant and in the past they were exported in the thousands and could be purchased very cheaply both in Europe and

A pair of Cobalt-winged Parakeets (*Brotogeris cyanoptera*).

*"Swift on the wing,
Brotogeris
Parakeets will make
good use of a
lengthy flight. Most
are quite hardy once
fully acclimatized,
although individuals
do seem to vary in
this respect."*

the USA. Nowadays far fewer reach the pet trade market and prices have consequently risen quite dramatically.

Were it not for their rather unattractive vocal talents, they might enjoy even greater popularity as household pets. As it is, they are not generally renowned for their powers of mimicry, although certain individuals will learn to repeat the odd word or two. They are more likely to learn to mimic the sounds of other birds and animals rather than the human voice.

As indicated by the bare area of skin around the lower mandible and on the sides of the face, these birds are avid fruit eaters in the wild and fruit should be a prominent feature of their diet in captivity. Few individuals will be prepared to even sample greenfood, although it should at least be offered from time to time. Nectar can be given occasionally and will usually prove acceptable.

Swift on the wing, *Brotogeris* Parakeets will make good use of a lengthy flight. Most are quite hardy once fully acclimatized, although individuals do seem to vary in this respect.

It is therefore a good idea to leave their nesting logs in position throughout the year, so that they can retire to them at night. Some will take full advantage of this cozier situation, while others may prefer to roost in the open.

Seldom does one see a brotogerid in anything less

than immaculate garb. Being enthusiastic bathers, they should always be provided with a source of clean water for bathing purposes, and they will usually be seen to take a dip on even the coldest winter day.

Breeding successes in captivity are very rare, partly on account of the fact that it is quite impossible to sex any of these birds by visual means.

Tovi Parakeet (*Brotogeris jugularis*)

Colloquially known as Bee-

Tovi Parakeet (Brotogeris jugularis). Young brotogerids have the same coloring as adults as soon as their feathers come in.

bees and sometimes called the Orange-chinned Parakeet, this species has long been the most commonly imported member of the group as far as the USA is concerned, where it enjoys enormous popularity as a pet.

In total length this species does not exceed 7 inches (18 cm). As the latter of its two alternative names implies, it is readily distinguishable from other members of the genus by the characteristic orange markings on the chin. It has no other bright colors, being predominantly green, darker above and paler below. There are tinges of blue on the crown, lower regions of the back, rump, and the uppermost surface of the tail.

There is a large patch of brown on the wings; the primary coverts are purple and the underwing coverts are olive. The bill is horn colored and the iris is chocolate brown. Youngsters differ very little from adults.

It is extremely common in many parts of its range and individuals are found alternately in small groups or very large flocks. Distribution stretches from western Mexico to northern Venezuela. In the wild these birds are sociable nest builders, with several pairs often nesting in the same tree.

Unfortunately, few breeding successes have been recorded in captivity and usually reproduction occurs only when a reasonable number of pairs are housed together in a colony. It is unlikely that success would occur with a

Tovi Parakeet.

single pair.

Four eggs form the average clutch and the incubation period is thought to be three and a half weeks. Youngsters make good pets if they can be taken young from the nest; at one time they were exported by the thousands, after being hand-reared by their captors before being sold to dealers.

Nowadays, with more and more of the South American countries placing limitations on exports, far fewer have come on to the avicultural scene.

Its voice can be a little off-putting at times, but generally the Tovi is one of the most attractive propositions as a pet among the more readily available members of the *Brotogeris* family.

Orange-flanked Parakeet (Brotogeris pyrrhopterus)
Alternatively known by the equally descriptive names of

Orange-winged and Grey-cheeked Parakeet, this is one of the most commonly available members of the tribe and has long enjoyed popular status as a pet, particularly in the USA.

It is readily distinguishable from other brotogerids by its brilliant orange underwing

The Tovi Parakeet has been hybridized with several of its genus mates.

Above and right:
**Orange-flanked
Parakeets
(*Brotogeris
pyrrhopterus*). In
the wild, this
species is often
seen near banana
plantations.**

they lack the bluish feathering on the crown and may be a little paler overall.

This species is more limited in its range than any other representative of the genus, being confined to the southwestern parts of Peru and western Ecuador, where it is reported to be quite common.

Again, at one time many thousands were exported annually, but far fewer are now departing from their countries of origin. Happily this species has proved more free-breeding than other members of the genus and many of those currently being offered for sale are captive-bred.

These little birds are of an extremely bold disposition and will readily challenge a

coverts, and it has a somewhat more solid-looking general appearance.

It is mainly bright green, and like the Tovi, this color scheme is arranged with darker shading on top and paler below. The forehead, chin, and cheeks are gray and there is a bluish tinge to the crown and primaries.

The eyes are dark brown, the beak horn colored and the legs and feet pinkish. Length is approximately 8 inches (20 cm). Youngsters closely resemble adults, although parrot two or three times their size and usually emerge unscathed! Their vocal talents can be quite harsh at times, but they are by no means as unpleasantly voiced as other members of the Conure family.

Countless numbers of these birds are kept as pets in the USA, often being completely hand-tame when they arrive at their final destination. If taken young from the nest and hand-reared, they are extremely trusting. They are not the best of mimics, although certain individuals will learn to repeat the odd word or two.

Tui Parakeet
(*Brotogeris sanctithomae*)

Generally considered to be the least vocal member of the

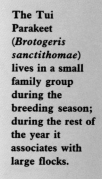

The Orange-flanked Parakeet may be the most popular brotogerid in captivity.

The Tui Parakeet (*Brotogeris sanctithomae*) lives in a small family group during the breeding season; during the rest of the year it associates with large flocks.

Tui Parakeet (*Brotogeris sanctithomae*). A cinnamon mutation of this species has been seen in captivity.

It is widely distributed throughout much of the Amazon basin. A much less commonly encountered subspecies, *B.s. takatsukasae*, occurs only in Brazil (close to the river Amazon). It is distinguished by the yellow streak immediately behind the eye.

In the wild both the nominate form and its subspecies may choose a hole in a tree for nesting purposes, but they are more likely to build in a termite mound. Perhaps it is the difficulty of recreating a natural nesting environment that has led to the lack of captive-breeding.

Surprisingly for a species which is common in the wild and which, until recently, was extensively exported, there is no account of its having produced youngsters in captivity.

It is not the most suitable member of the *Brotogeris* group to keep as a pet, as individuals tend to be nervous and may never gain the full confidence needed to become completely tame. It is doubtful that any bird would ever become a competent mimic.

All-green Parakeet
(*Brotogeris tirica*)

In spite of its common status in the wild, few examples have ever been exported and this species remains the "mystery man" among the *Brotogeris* Parakeets. Perhaps its lack of any bright colors has partly accounted for it being neglected in favor of its more attractively garbed cousins.

genus, it may be thought of as one of the most suitable candidates for pet status among the *Brotogeris* Parakeets for that reason alone.

Unique among its genus mates, it has a chestnut brown bill rather than one which is horn colored. The forehead and the crown are marked with yellow. In overall coloration it is dark green above and a slightly lighter green below. The underside of the tail is olive colored. The iris is a yellowish shade of white.

"All-green" is a term which does not entirely do this species justice, as its basically green coloration is tinged with blue on the nape, a dusky shade on the underside of the tail and brown on the upperwing coverts.

The bill is horn colored, although it is a little darker at the base than in other members of the genus. The iris is dark brown. Total length is 9 inches (23 cm), making this species the largest of the *Brotogeris* Parakeets, although half of this length is accounted for by the bird's tail.

In youngsters, the tail is much shorter and the bill is of a darker shade. The primaries and secondaries are tinged with blue.

The All-green is very common indeed in its native habitat and is even to be found nesting in city parks and gardens throughout eastern Brazil. It is therefore strange to report that it has never been freely exported and it was probably more readily available to aviculturists living a century ago than to those who might wish to add a pair of these birds to their collection today.

Four eggs would seem to be the norm and the incubation period is 26 days. Youngsters remain in the nest for about six weeks.

No details have been recorded as to how individuals have adapted to existence as household pets. Not the most confiding member of the *Brotogeris* family, there are certainly others which more readily spring to mind as suitable subjects for taming.

White-winged Parakeet (*Brotogeris versicolorus*)

Otherwise known as the Yellow-winged Parakeet and sometimes incorrectly referred to as the Canary-winged Parakeet, it is hardly surprising that mistakes are made regarding its identification, as there is

The White-winged Parakeet (*Brotogeris versicolorus versicolorus*) is the nominate form of its species.

White-winged
Parakeet
(*Brotogeris
versicolorus
versicolorus*)
displaying the
white and yellow
coloration of its
wing.

*"Many White-wings
enjoy pet status and
they are certainly
among the most
suitable subjects for
hand-taming."*

really very little to distinguish this bird from its equally popular subspecies.

The basic coloration is green, although this is of a grayer shade than in the Canary-wing, especially on the forehead. Another distinguishing feature is the bluish coloring around the eyes. The yellow wing patch is not of such a bright yellow coloration as is apparent on the Canary-wing. The beak is horn colored and the legs are pinkish gray. Total length is 9 inches (23 cm). Youngsters may be identified by the smaller amount of coloring in the wings.

Distribution is from eastern Ecuador through to northeastern Peru. A few isolated pockets of habitation

have occurred elsewhere, possibly as a result of individuals which have been kept as pets making a successful bid for freedom.

In the early years of the 20th century this species was rarely imported, but now it ranks as one of the most common members of the genus. It is therefore surprising that there are very few records of its having bred in captivity. Doubtless its breeding pattern would follow much the same lines as other *Brotogeris* Parakeets.

Many White-wings enjoy pet status and they are certainly among the most suitable subjects for hand-taming. It may even be possible to teach a pet to learn the odd word or short phrase.

During courtship, the male White-winged Parakeet faithfully feeds its partner.

Canary-winged
Parakeet
(*Brotogeris
versicolorus
chiriri*). This
subspecies is
brighter in color
than the
nominate White-
winged Parakeet.

A pair of Canary-
winged
Parakeets.

Canary-winged Parakeet (*Brotogeris versicolorus chiriri*)

This parakeet, with its brighter, far more distinct coloring, is a much more attractive little bird than the foregoing, with which it is so often confused. Many thousands have been purchased as pets over the years and it remains one of the most popular small parrots, especially in the USA.

It is a rich light green color, being darker above and lighter below. The yellow wing patches are much brighter than those of *B. versicolorus*. The bill is a light buff brown and the iris is a darker shade of the same color. Length varies from 8½–

9 inches (22–23 cm). Youngsters are very similar, although they lack the brightness of yellow in the wings.

It has a fairly wide range, being distributed through northern Argentina and Paraguay to northern and eastern Bolivia and southern parts of Brazil.

Although these birds make excellent pets, they really need to be kept in an aviary for one to be able to appreciate their highly active natures and for the quiet beauty of their plumage to be seen to advantage.

Unfortunately, successful breeding attempts in captivity have been very few indeed. Clutch size may vary from three to six and the usual incubation period is 26 days. Youngsters remain in the nest for up to eight weeks.

Highly recommended as a pet, most people will be quickly taken in by the endearing personalities of these cheerfully mannered little birds. One in my own collection soon learned to repeat his name (Peter) and

became a real character, always insisting on being paid attention whenever one passed his aviary, flying to me immediately in the hope that I had a sunflower seed or other tidbit hidden about my person.

As well as making superb pets, Canary-wings always seem to be particularly sleek of feather (once they have undergone a molt after exportation and a period of quarantine).

An individual, or better still a pair, will therefore make an excellent choice for exhibition purposes, seldom looking anything less than immaculate. My own pair once took second in their class at the National Exhibition of Cage and Aviary Birds, when it was held at London's Alexandra Palace, and won best Foreign Bird and Parrot-like awards on numerous occasions.

GENUS *CYANOLISEUS*

This genus has but a sole representative, the extremely attractive and showy Patagonian Conure, of which three subspecies are known to aviculturists. It is the largest of the Conures—individuals measure between 17–20 inches (43–51 cm) in total length—although it is in no way cumbersome.

A group of these birds makes a particularly striking exhibit in a zoo or bird garden, where they are best able to demonstrate their powerful voices without causing undue disturbance.

A pair of Slender-billed Conures (*Enicognathus leptorhynchus*). Members of this genus are closely related to the genus *Pyrrhura*.

Patagonian Conure (*Cyanoliseus patagonus*). Members of this species are also known as Burrowing Parrots.

Unlike most Conures, the Patagonian and its subspecies has a feathered cere.

The three subspecies—the Andean Patagonian (*C.p. andinus*), the Greater Patagonian (*C.p. byroni*) and the Lesser Patagonian (*C.p. patagonus*)—are very similar in appearance and can be treated in exactly the same manner. It is therefore proposed not to deal with them separately, except to describe how each differs in physical appearance to the nominate form.

Patagonian Conure (*Cyanoliseus patagonus*)

Unfortunately, many Patagonian Conures are subject to a great deal of persecution throughout their range; in some regions the young chicks are regarded as a great delicacy for human consumption, and this

destructive prediliction has further added to the problems which beset this species in the wild.

Those with an interest in maintaining these birds in captivity may prove to be their saving grace, especially as individual pairs are not normally too difficult to persuade to go to nest. It may, however, be out of the question to keep Patagonians if one has neighbors living in close proximity. In spite of

their largely unattractive vocal talents, the Patagonians are of extremely pleasing coloration and are regarded as a most desirable addition to many collections.

In the nominate race the head, neck, and back are dark olive-brown interspersed with feathers of a more true green coloration. There are a few flecks of white on the upper regions of the breast, which is otherwise grayish-brown, as is the bird's throat.

A breeding pair of Patagonian Conures. The male is the bird with more red on its thighs.

A trio of Thick-billed Parakeets (*Rhynchopsitta pachyrhyncha*). Members of this genus are said to fall between the Conures and Macaws in taxonomy.

"The Andean Patagonian Conure displays the most distinctly marked differences to the nominate form . . ."

The lower regions of the back, rump and uppertail coverts are olive-yellow. The most striking features are the extensive areas of red and yellow across the bird's abdomen. The wings are olive-green, with the primaries colored blue.

The tail is similarly olive-green, with the under surfaces brown and the undertail coverts olive-yellow. There is a slight bluish tinge to much of the bird's tail. An encircling band of bare white flesh surrounds the eye and the iris is likewise white. The beak is black in adults, whereas in youngsters the upper mandible is off-white and the iris gray.

The Andean Patagonian Conure displays the most distinctly marked differences to the nominate form, having little or no yellow on the abdomen and far less extensive areas of red. Its plumage is generally duller. It does not vary in size from *C. patagonus*.

On the other hand, the areas of red and yellow on the breast of the Greater Patagonian Conure are even brighter and more extensive than is apparent in *C. patagonus*. Occasionally the whitish markings on the upper parts of the breast form an unbroken band across the bird's chest. It is the largest of all the Conures, measuring approximately 20 inches (53 cm) in total length.

The smaller Lesser Patagonian Conure differs from the nominate race only in having the white markings confined to the outermost parts of the upper breast regions. Length is 17–18 inches (43–46 cm).

The Patagonian Conures are found in central Chile, northern and central Argentina and parts of Uruguay. The Lesser is confined to the central regions of Argentina, occasionally extending its range into Uruguay. The Greater is restricted to the foothills of the Andes and the Andean occurs only in the mountainous regions of northwestern Argentina.

Although the best results of a captive-breeding program are likely to be induced by a policy of restricting one pair to a flight, colony breeding has proved successful on a number of occasions in the UK, Germany, Czechoslovakia, USA, and elsewhere.

In their natural habitat, Patagonian Conures will excavate suitable nesting sites in sandstone cliffs, and many zoos have successfully emulated this environmental aid to encourage nest-building operations. Nevertheless, individual pairs will adapt to a large nest-box or nesting log.

In display the cock bird will draw himself up to his full height and make loud snapping sounds with his beak, which the female often copies. Her mate will then strut along the perch in an exaggerated manner. Copulation usually follows this show of bravado.

Three or four eggs form the average clutch and their 24- or 25-day incubation period will be undertaken by the female, with no assistance being offered by her mate, who seldom enters the nest until there are chicks to be fed. Youngsters will vacate the nest at approximately eight weeks old, at which point they will continue to be fed by their father for another two to three weeks.

Since they are not really suited to a caged existence, Patagonian Conures are not to be recommended as pets. A fairly large aviary, measuring at least 15–18 ft (4.5–5.1 m) in length, is necessary to display these birds to full advantage.

Artist's rendering of a Lesser Patagonian Conure

A pair of Nanday Conures (*Nandayus nenday*). In general, Nanday Conures will remain with the same mate for life.

In general, the Nanday Conure becomes a tame and affectionate pet if acclimated properly.

GENUS *NANDAYUS*

It is difficult to fathom how this separate genus could be formed simply to accommodate its sole representative—the Nanday Conure—as only minute anatomical differences distinguish this species from the *Aratingas*.

Nanday Conure (*Nandayus nenday*)

Otherwise descriptively known as the Black-headed or Black-masked Conure, this species is common both in the wild and as an avicultural subject. It has much to recommend it, being extremely free-breeding—pairs will readily go to nest kept singly or in a colony, where they tend to be particularly raucous.

As can be ascertained from its alternative names, the head, nape and facial areas are predominantly black, interspersed with the odd green feather or two. The major remaining part of the plumage is apple green, more yellowish towards the underparts, lower regions of the back, rump, and underwing coverts.

The throat and upper regions of the breast are

Many experts
feel that the
Nanday Conure
should be
included in the
genus *Aratinga*.

"Common throughout their range, Nandays can be found in Bolivia, Brazil, northern Argentina and Paraguay."

tinged with blue and the upper surface of the tail is similarly defined. Many of the outer webs of the flight feathers are also blue. It has distinctive red thighs, which give individuals the appearance of wearing trousers. A narrow encircling band of whitish skin surrounds the eye, the iris of which is dark brown. The bill is black. Overall length is 12 inches (31 cm).

Young birds closely resemble their parents, except that they have a much shorter tail (in adults this feature accounts for half of the total length). Once the tail has grown, it is very difficult to distinguish juveniles from adults.

Common throughout their range, Nandays can be found in Bolivia, Brazil, northern parts of Argentina and Paraguay. Flocks can number several hundred individuals and can prove quite annoying to farmers.

The first importations of this species occurred over 100 years ago, and since then there has always been a steady flow coming into Europe and the USA. As a result they have long remained one of the most instantly recognizable and cheapest members of the Conure family.

Although pairs will usually breed quite readily, the large numbers being regularly imported and available at little cost have meant that there have been few serious attempts to establish breeding colonies. Prices have risen a little of late and this has had the fortunate effect of making breeders take this species a little more seriously.

Three-month-old Nanday Conure (*Nandayus nenday*), left, with a six-month-old "Nansun" Conure, a Nanday/Sun Conure (*Nandayus nenday/Aratinga solstitialis*) hybrid, right.

Adult female Nanday Conure.

Four or five eggs form the average clutch and are incubated by the female alone for the 26-day period before the chicks begin to emerge. Upon hatching, Nanday chicks are completely naked, but they soon develop a sparse amount of whitish colored down. Youngsters remain in the nest for up to eight weeks.

In spite of being easy to feed, young Nandays are extremely vociferous in their demands even at this age, and those who are experienced at this practice may regard them as their least favorite subject for adoption and subsequent hand-rearing. However, if they are fed in this manner during their formative weeks, they will make tame and affectionate pets, but their voices will grate on even the most insensitive ears at times.

GENUS *PYRRHURA*

This group contains the smaller members of the Conure family. All of its representatives are easy to cater to and can be recommended to the beginner and experienced aviculturist alike. They have exquisite personalities, making them eminently suitable as pets, and most will be quite prepared to go to nest outside their countries of origin. Unfortunately, of the 16 species represented in this genus, only half are reasonably well-known to aviculturists, with the Red-bellied being the most frequently imported. In all species, male and female are identical.

Pyrrhuras have a natural inquisitiveness which will lead them to investigate all manner of foods, but this curiosity will also lead them to discover the small opening in the wire-netting of their enclosure, through which to make their escape. Beware! These South American Houdinis are escape artists without parallel!

Although nowhere near as strident as members of other genera within the Conure group, there are times when their voices can be somewhat tiresome to listen to for any period of time. However, their call notes are really no noisier than those at the more shrill end of a Cockatiel's scale.

Breeding has been attempted on the colony system, but it is not altogether successful. Individuals which may have agreed for many months can suddenly turn on one another and commit murder most foul!

Generally *Pyrrhuras* are not as strenuously destructive as many of the aforementioned species. A suitable aviary need only measure 8–10 ft (2.4–3 m) in length, and most pairs will adapt to a variety of nesting facilities. Youngsters are among the easiest of

Artist's rendering of a trio of *Pyrrhura* Conures. *Top:* Black-tailed Conure (*Pyrrhura melanura*). *Center:* Green-cheeked Conure (*Pyrrhura molinae*). *Bottom:* Painted Conure (*Pyrrhura picta*).

parrot chicks to adopt for hand-rearing purposes and will make excellent pets if treated in this manner from the outset.

Red-bellied Conure (*Pyrrhura frontalis*)

Occasionally referred to by dealers as the Scaly-breasted Conure, this is undoubtedly the most frequently encountered member of the genus. Although seldom imported in the early years of the 20th century, since the 1920s regular consignments have reached the USA and Europe.

In typical *Pyrrhura* fashion, the olive-green feathers of the upper breast regions are heavily scalloped, being edged with a bright golden-yellow. The head is maroon colored and there is a patch of the same hue on the bird's abdomen. The crown, nape, and cheeks are dark green and the ear coverts are a light

buff color.

The upper surface of the tail is green at the base, becoming red towards the center; the underside of the tail is a darker shade of red. A prominent circle of white surrounds the eye. The beak, iris, and feet are all black. Length is 11 inches (28 cm). On emerging from the nest youngsters closely resemble their parents.

The natural habitat of this species is southeastern Brazil, where it is locally common. Azara's Conure (*P.f. chiripepe*), a subspecies of *P. frontalis*, extends as far as Paraguay. It differs from the nominate race in lacking the maroon on

Red-bellied Conure (*Pyrrhura frontalis*). This species is one of the most frequently imported members of its genus.

Azara's Conure (*Pyrrhura frontalis chiripepe*), a subspecies of the Red-bellied Conure.

the lower parts of the breast and having the upper surface of the tail golden-olive and lacking the red central markings.

Another subspecies, the very rare Krieg's Conure (*P.f. kriegi*), also has the upper surface of the tail green, although in this instance it is narrowly tipped with blood-red.

It has only been since the 1970s that pairs of Red-bellied Conures have been allowed to go to nest in reasonably large numbers, as this species was once so commonly and cheaply imported that few breeders considered it worthy of serious effort.

An average clutch size is five eggs. The incubation period is 26 days and the young remain in the nest for 28 days before fledging. Although closely resembling adults, they may be slightly

duller in coloring. Most Red-bellied Conures will prove extremely attentive parents, and pairs have been employed from time to time to act as foster parents to less free-breeding members of the *Pyrrhura* genus.

Hybrids have occurred between many of the more freely imported members of the group, most frequently with the Black-tailed Conure (*P. melanura*).

The potential of this species as a pet subject has not been fully explored but, like virtually all of the species covered in this book, there is little doubt that, if taken young enough from the nest, an individual would soon become tame and confiding.

White-eared Conure (*Pyrrhura leucotis*)

One of the first of the *Pyrrhuras* to be exported in large numbers, these birds have been quite freely available to aviculturists since the latter part of the 19th century. However, more recently they have become far less readily available and consequently prices have risen steeply. This is unfortunate, as this is a most attractive species, having the forehead, cheeks, and lores a rich chestnut brown color. Small amounts of blue are featured on the cheeks and on the nape. The lores are maroon colored and the ear coverts are a pale shade of buff.

The neck, throat, and upper regions of the breast are

A pair of White-eared Conures (*Pyrrhura leucotis*). In the wild, members of this species have been known to eat ants.

The Red-bellied
Conure
(*Pyrrhura
frontalis*) has
been hybridized
with the White-
eared Conure.

Artist's rendering of a White-eared Conure (*Pyrrhura leucotis*). Many White-eared Conures do not reproduce until they are two years old.

dusky-brown or green, with the normal scalloped effect typical of this genus achieved by the bordering edge of grayish-buff feathering. A patch of maroon extends from the lower part of the back to the uppertail coverts and there is a similarly colored irregular patch on the bird's abdomen.

The tail is maroon above, green at its base and orange-red on the under surface. Both the bill and the iris are brown. Length is 8½ inches (21 cm). Youngsters closely resemble adults.

This species occurs principally in eastern Brazil and northern Venezuela. These areas are approximately 200 miles apart, so the two populations are isolated.

One of the most attractive members of the *Pyrrhura* group, this species was bred more frequently in the early part of this century rather than in latter years.

It is not unusual for a clutch to number up to eight eggs. Indeed, such large clutches are the norm and it would be more remarkable for a hen to be found brooding only three or four eggs. Youngsters remain in the nest for seven or eight weeks.

The White-eared Conure's attributes as a pet have not so far been recorded, but, no doubt, youngsters have proved themselves as pets in the past.

Black-tailed Conure (Pyrrhura melanura)

Confusingly, this species is also known as the Maroon-tailed Conure, on account of the fact that the tail is jet black above and a dark maroon color below. Four subspecies are known to exist and all have marked differences in coloration.

In the nominate race, the forehead is brown and the crown has a mottled appearance on account of the feathers having green edges. The upper regions of the breast are brownish-green, with the feathers displaying lighter edges, lending a scaled effect.

There are a few scattered maroon feathers on the bird's abdomen and the remainder of the underparts are of a dark green coloration. The primaries are red tipped with yellow. The bill is light brown and an area of bare white skin surrounds the eye. The iris is dark brown. Length is 10 inches (25 cm). Youngsters closely resemble their elders, although the markings on the breast may be somewhat lighter.

The first of the subspecies, P.m. berlepschi, differs from the above in having the ear coverts a much lighter shade of green and a yellow tinge to the green upper parts. The maroon patch on the abdomen is far more distinct.

The second of the subspecies, P.m. chapmani, has the upper breast regions dark brown, broadly edged with white. Little maroon is apparent on the abdomen and the ear coverts are partly green. However, there is less green on the crown and at the base of the tail. There is also a bluish shading to the green plumage around the nape.

Another of the subspecies, P.m. pacifica, has the distinction of being the only Conure to be found west of the Andes range of mountains. It lacks both the patch of maroon on the abdomen and the yellow on the wing coverts. The upper breast regions are a dull green color, with the feathers thinly edged with a quiet shade of pink. The area of naked skin surrounding the eye is gray as opposed to white and thus far less distinct. It is fractionally shorter in overall length.

The last of the subspecies, P.m. souancei, displays a much more extensive area of red on the primaries and lacks the yellow. The scaling on the upper parts of the breast is more readily discernible, as the feathers are much more broadly edged.

The nominate form has a wide distribution ranging across Colombia, northeastern Peru, Brazil and the southern areas of Venezuela.

The species was not

"Confusingly, this species is also known as the Maroon-tailed Conure, on account of the fact that the tail is jet black above and a dark maroon color below."

Breeding pair of Green-cheeked Conures *(Pyrrhura molinae molinae)*. The male is facing the camera.

Adult male subspecies of the Green-cheeked Conure *(Pyrrhura molinae restricta)*.

although the markings around the throat tend to be fainter and the legs and feet are considerably darker.

On account of their nervousness and general lack of confidence, these birds cannot be recommended to the would-be pet owner.

Green-cheeked Conure (Pyrrhura molinae)

Otherwise known as Molina's Conure, this species resembles the aviculturally much more common Red-bellied (*P. frontalis*), with which it is often confused.

In appearance it can only be distinguished from the Red-bellied in that the crown and nape are brown and the forehead is more reddish-

commonly imported in any of its forms until the late 1960s, when large numbers began to be offered by dealers. Individuals tend to be extremely nervous, especially when newly imported, and this probably partly accounts for the fact that the Black-tailed Conure has never built up a popular following, despite its comparative availability of late.

Breeding attempts in captivity are fairly rare, although pairs have gone to nest on a number of occasions. Four or five eggs form the average clutch size. Youngsters emerge from the brood chamber at approximately seven weeks of age, whereupon they closely resemble their parents,

brown and the cheeks are green. Length is likewise 10 inches (26 cm). Youngsters are generally of a much paler coloration overall.

Its natural habitat is Brazil, although little is known about its breeding habits either in the wild or in captivity.

Its potential as a pet would be much the same as that of the closely related Red-bellied Conure.

Pearly Conure
(Pyrrhura perlata)

Inquisitive by nature, these birds have the most amazing talent for escape and will soon find the tiniest hole in the wire-mesh of their enclosure through which to make their bid for freedom. They will investigate new foods avidly and any suitable nesting receptacle placed in their flight will soon be an object of their unbridled curiosity.

Not of a particularly bright coloration, their mainly dull feathering is relieved only by the scarlet underwing coverts. Otherwise the forehead and crown are a dull gray and the throat is dark gray, edged with a lighter shade of the same color. The feathers on the upper regions of the breast are bordered with blue, thus creating a scaled effect.

Blue is also the color of the nape, tail coverts and the feathers surrounding the vent. The lower parts of the breast,

A friendly, hand-reared Green-cheeked Conure (*Pyrrhura molinae molinae*).

Artist's rendering of a White-eared Conure (*Pyrrhura leucotis*) and a Pearly Conure (*Pyrrhura perlata*).

A pair of Crimson-bellied Conures (*Pyrrhura rhodogaster*). In the wild, these bright little birds remain absolutely silent when alarmed.

avicultural point of view. It is very similar in coloration to the nominate form, differing only to the extent of having green underwing coverts.

Although never imported in very great numbers, individuals are occasionally available. Only in the early 1960s did the first breedings occur in Great Britain and the USA.

Four eggs form the average clutch, and the incubation period can once again be calculated at 26 days. Youngsters remain in the nest until they are between seven and eight weeks old. Taken from their parents at this stage, there is every chance that they would make good pets.

wings, and back are dark green. The uppermost surface of the tail is maroon, while the underside is blackish. The beak, legs, and feet are black, as is the iris. Total length is 9½ inches (24 cm). Only in the paler colored bill do youngsters differ from adults.

Distribution is throughout northeastern Brazil. Strangely, the principle subspecies, *P.p. anerythra,* is considered to be the more common of the two birds, especially from the

Two other subspecies are known to exist, but very little is understood about them. The Miritiba Pearly Conure (*P.p. coerulescens*) has only a small local distribution and the same can be said of the Para Pearly Conure (*P.p. pseudoperlata*).

Painted Conure
(*Pyrrhura picta*)

Aviculturally rare until the early 1970s, this is a most attractive little Conure, of which five subspecies are known to exist.

It has a black crown, and the forehead and the lower regions of the cheeks blue and a thin band of the same color runs across the nape. The blue of the cheeks merges into maroon, the ear coverts are gray and the throat and the sides of the neck are dark brown or blackish.

The typical scaled effect of the throat and upper breast regions is produced by being edged with varying shades of light gray, brown, and olive. A patch of maroon extends from the lower part of the back to the uppertail coverts and through to the abdomen. The bend of the wing is scarlet and the primaries are edged with blue. The tail is maroon above and brownish-red below. Length is 9½ inches (24 cm).

Youngsters can be distinguished from the fact that the bend of the wing is not wholly scarlet, being interspersed with green feathers.

The first of the subspecies, the Santarem Conure (*P.p. amazonum*) has the bend of

the wing entirely green, and the four central tail feathers are also thinly edged with green. The forehead is pale blue to a point just beyond the eye. The ear coverts are buff colored.

Another subspecies, *P.p. caeruleiceps*, is immediately recognizable in having the

Painted Conure (*Pyrrhura picta*). Members of this species prefer access to a daily bath.

Adult male
Painted Conure
(*Pyrrhura picta*).

"*Very few breedings
have taken place
and little is known
about the
reproductive habits
of this species
[Painted Conure]
in captivity. Its pet
potential is similarly
unrecorded.*"

Opposite: Adult
pair of Painted
Conures.
During the
breeding season,
the male will
spend most of his
time guarding
the entrance to
the hollow where
the nest is found.

entire crown dull blue,
blending into a dusky shade
on the nape. The cheeks and
lores are brown. The
scalloping of the throat
feathers is achieved by the
addition of a dirty white color
bordering the outer webs of
the plumage.

The third subspecies, *P.p.
microtera*, differs very little
from *P.p. amazonum* except
that it is slightly smaller and
has less blue on the forehead.
It is also a more dusky shade
of green overall.

Next we have *P.p.
orinocensis*, which differs only
from the nominate race in
displaying a paler colored
crown and having less
pronounced scalloping on the
throat.

Finally there is the
Jaraquiel Conure (*P.p.
subandina*), which has the ear
coverts yellowish-brown and
the iris straw colored. The
primaries are blue tipped
with black.

In all its subspecies the
Painted Conure has a very
wide distribution from the
Guyanas to Venezuela through
to northern Bolivia,
southeastern Peru and
northwestern Colombia.

Very few breedings have
taken place and little is
known about the reproductive
habits of this species in
captivity. Its pet potential is
similarly unrecorded.

Conservation

Opposite:
**Canary-winged
Parakeet
(*Brotogeris
versicolorus
chiriri*) and
Petz's Conure
(*Aratinga
canicularis*).**

**As more and
more
restrictions are
placed upon the
exportation of
wild Conures,
hobbyists will
rely increasingly
on captive-bred
stock.**

Unfortunately, all the species covered in this book are suffering from the destruction of their natural habitats and from over-trapping, particularly in the past.

It may be a case of "too little—too late," but nowadays South American governments are beginning to realize the follies of previous administrations in allowing such a trade to continue unchecked for so long.

The result of this realization has, in many instances, led to a limitation of the numbers being exported and sometimes a total ban. Numbers of Conures being exported to the USA and Europe are fewer than ever before and the situation is unlikely to improve.

Species which were once commonly and inexpensively available from dealers' establishments are now very rarely seen, and many of those which are offered for sale command quite high prices.

Such days are never likely to return, and in some ways that is not altogether a bad thing. When these delightful little parrots were so readily and cheaply available, few breeders ever took the trouble to provide them with sufficient incentive to go to nest.

Among the smaller parrots, the breeding potential of captive Conures has been ignored for far too long. One problem experienced in the past was simply not being able to sex them, but with the

Jandaya Conure
(*Aratinga jandaya*).

"What is needed is a concentrated effort by large numbers of enthusiasts to increase captive populations of these birds by second and third generation breedings."

Opposite:
Finsch's Conure
(*Aratinga finschi*).

advent of surgical sexing, this should no longer be any excuse for anyone not to make an attempt to establish true pairs.

Hand-rearing methods have come a long way in the past decade or so and there are a number of excellent books solely devoted to this subject. Hand-rearing *is* a very demanding undertaking, but also a wholly rewarding one.

Time may be running out for many Conures in the wild, which fact bestows a responsibility on every keeper of these birds to do his or her bit towards their conservation by encouraging as many pairs to go to nest as possible. Isolated breeding achievements, albeit worthy in themselves, cannot lead to the ultimate preservation of a species.

What is needed is a concentrated effort by large numbers of enthusiasts to increase captive populations of these birds by second and third generation breedings. Only then can they be assured

of a future.

South America currently supports a greater variety of parrot species than any other continent in the world. Indeed, the number of species represented compares favorably with that of the rest of the world put together.

How long that situation will continue one can only hazard a guess. However, it does not take much to assume that at least some of that number are unlikely to remain well into the 21st century, unless man takes a hand in preventing the wholesale destruction of their habitat. Here aviculturists have a chance to prove that they are not merely consumers of the world's bird-life, but that they can also play an important role in helping to preserve certain species from extinction.

Both as aviary birds and household pets, Conures have delighted their owners for many years. Now is the time for their keepers to repay that debt of gratitude.

Illustration Index

Azara's Conure, 125
Black-tailed Conure, 124
Blue and Gold Macaw, 10
Blue-crowned Conure, 22, 32, 66, 71, 82, 89
Brown-throated Conure, 60, 85, 89
Cactus Conure, 27, 61, 88, 89
Canary-winged Parakeet, 57, 70, 81, 104, 114, 137
Cobalt-winged Parakeet, 7, 45, 47, 51, 72, 78, 104, 105
Cockatiel, 10
Crimson-bellied Conure, 132
Cuban Conure, 89
Dusky-headed Conure, 12, 16, 89, 102, 103
Finsch's Conure, 18, 28, 30, 35, 41, 84, 138
Golden-capped Conure, 21, 48, 82, 89
Golden-crowned Conure, 6, 10, 12, 15, 76, 86, 87, 89
Golden-winged Parakeet, 48
Green-cheeked Conure, 14, 124, 130, 131
Green Conure, 42, 85, 89
Jandaya Conure, 9, 10, 12, 17, 23, 24, 41, 96, 97, 138
Lesser Patagonian Conure, 119
Mitred Conure, 13, 37, 84
Nanday Conure, 16, 18, 25, 31, 44, 53, 54, 76, 77, 79, 120, 121, 123

"Nansun" Conure, 64, 122
Olive-throated Conure, 84, 89
Orange-flanked Parakeet, 8, 40, 45, 50, 51, 55, 59, 62, 66, 70, 79, 108, 109
Painted Conure, 124, 133, 134
Patagonian Conure, 56, 116, 117
Pearly Conure, 132
Petz's Conure, 9, 12, 36, 81, 89, 90, 91
Queen of Bavaria's Conure, 12, 26, 52, 93, 94, 95
Red-bellied Conure, 14, 50, 125, 127
Red-fronted Conure, 85, 89
Red-masked Conure, 18, 25, 56, 67, 68, 89, 92
Scarlet Macaw, 10
Slender-billed Conure, 81, 115
Sun Conure, 11, 17, 33, 65, 66, 99, 100, 101
Thick-billed Parakeet, 58, 118
Tovi Parakeet, 22, 29, 74, 75, 106
Tui Parakeet, 104, 109, 110
Tuipara Parakeet, 104
White-eared Conure, 126, 128, 132
White-eyed Conure, 98
White-winged Parakeet, 111, 112, 113

Index

African Grey Parrot, 47, 59
Ailments and Diseases, 53–61
Alexandra Palace, 115
All-green Parakeet, *110*, 111
Amazon basin, 102, 110
Amazon parrot, 7, 47, 59, 104
Amazon river, 94, 110
Andean Patagonian Conure, 116, *118*
Andes mountains, 119, 130
Aratinga, 8, 10, 11, 26, 32, 64, *81–85*, *82*, *83*, 91, 94, 95, 96, 99, 102, 103, 120
Aratinga aurea, 86
Aratinga cactorum, 88
Aratinga canicularis, *88*
Aratinga chloroptera, 98
Aratinga erythrogenys, *92*
Aratinga guarouba, *93*
Aratinga jandaya, *96*
Aratinga leucophthalmus, *98*
Aratinga solstitialis, *99*
Aratinga weddellii, *102*
Argentina, 86, 99, 114, 119, 122
Ascaridia columbae, 56
Aureomycin, 60
Australian Parakeet, 56, 63, 64
Aviary panels, 31
Azara's Conure, *125*
Bathing, 106
Beak trimming, 56
Bee-bee Parakeet, 106
Blackberries, 39
Black currants, 38
Black-headed Conure, 120
Black-masked Conure, 120
Black-tailed Conure, 126, *129*, 130
Bolivia, 86, 102, 114, 122, 134
Brazil, 86, 94, 101, 102, 110, 111, 114, 122, 125, 128, 130, 131, 132
Breeding, 63–70
Breeding cycle, 64
Brooder, 74, 75, 76, 77
—temperature, 75, 76
Brotogeris, 11, 81, *104–106*, 105, 107, 110, 111, 112
Brotogeris jugularis, 106
Brotogeris pyrrhopterus, 107
Brotogeris sanctithomae, 109
Brotogeris sanctithomae takatsukasae, 110
Brotogeris tirica, 110
Brotogeris versicolorus, *111*, 114
Brotogeris versicolorus chiriri, *114*
Brown bread, 39
Buckwheat, 36
Budgerigar, 21
Burns, 74
Cactus Conure, 88
Cage placement, 44
Cage size, 18
Canary seed, 36
Canary-winged Parakeet, 11, 111, 112, *114*, 115
Candling eggs, 68
Catch-net, 50, 51
Central America, 90
Cereals, 39
Cheese, 39
Chile, 119
Clipping claws, 55
Clutch size, 64, 85, 87, 93, 95, 97, 99, 103, 107, 111, 114, 119, 123, 126, 128, 130, 132
Cockatiel, 21, 67, 102, 124
Colombia, 99, 102, 130, 134
Concrete flooring, 30
Conservation, 137–138
Cork, 69
Costa Rica, 90

Cuttlefish bone, 41
Cyanoliseus, 11, *115–116*
Cyanoliseus patagonus, *116*
Cyanoliseus patagonus andinus, 116
Cyanoliseus patagonus byroni, 116
Cyanoliseus patagonus patagonus, 116
Dog biscuits, 39
Dusky-headed Conure, 8, *102*, 103
Ecuador, 92, 102, 108, 112
Egg-binding, 61
Everyday foods, 39
Eye disease, 60
Feather plucking, 59
Feeding, 35–41
Fertility, of eggs, 67, 68
Flight doors, 32
Floor covering, 20
Food bowls, 21, 22
Foster parents, 70
Fruits, 38
General Care, 43–51
Golden Conure, 93
Golden-crowned Conure, 8, 18, *86*, 87, 88, 89
Gooseberries, 38
Grass Parakeet, 21
Greater Golden-crowned Conure, 88
Greater Patagonian Conure, 17, 116, *118*
Green Conure, 98
Green-cheeked Conure, 8, *130*
Greenfood, 37
Grey-cheeked Parakeet, 107
Grit, 40
Guyanas, 101, 134
Halfmoon Conure, 88
Hand-rearing, 59, 70
Hand-rearing, 73–79
Hand-rearing, 103, 123, 125, 138, 138
Hand-rearing diet, 77, 78
Hard-boiled egg, 39
Hemp seed, 36
Hispaniolan Conure, 98
Hospital cage, 48, 54, 61, 74
—temperature, 54, 61
Housing, 17–32
Hybridization, 86, 88, 97, 126

Illness, signs of, 53
Incubation, 69
Incubation period, 64, 85, 97, 101, 103, 107, 111, 114, 119, 123, 126, 132
Infra-red light, 54
Iodine, 61
Jandaya Conure, 8, 88, *96*, 97, 100
Jaraquiel Conure, *134*
Jealousy, 13
Krieg's Conure, *126*
Lesser Patagonian Conure, 116, *118*
Linseed, 36
Loose droppings, 53
Lovebird, 104
Macaw, 7, 59, 81, 93, 95
Maroon-tailed Conure, 129
Mashed potato, 39
Mebendazole, 59
Mexico, 106
Milk, 39
Millet sprays, 35, 78
Mimicry, 45, 47, 109
Miritiba Pearly Conure, *133*
Misting, 43, 66
Molina's Conure, 130
Monkey chow, 39
Mung beans, 37
Nanday Conure, 88, 98, *120*
Nandayus, 11, 81, *120*, 122, 123
Nandayus nenday, 120
National Exhibition of Cage and Aviary Birds, 115
Nectar, 105
Nest-box, 28, 30, 50, 65, 66, 67, 69
Nest lining, 65, 66, 69
Oats, 36
Orange-chinned Parakeet, 106
Orange-flanked Conure, 88
Orange-flanked Parakeet, *107*
Orange-fronted Conure, 7
Orange-winged Parakeet, 107
Outside aviary, 24–30, 47
—lighting, 48
—size, 25
Overgrown claws, 55
Painted Conure, *133*, 134
Para Pearly Conure, *133*
Paraguay, 86, 99, 114, 122, 125

Parasitic worms, 56
Patagonian Conure, 8, 11, 25, 115, *116*, 117, 119
Peach-fronted Conure, 86
Peanuts, 36
Pearly Conure, *131*
Pelleted foods, 39
Perching, 22
Peru, 92, 102, 108, 112, 130, 134
Petz's Conure, 7, 8, 86, *88*, 89, 90
"Probe-lite," 68
Purchasing seed, 40
Pyrrhura, 8, 10, 11, 26, 32, 38, 64, 65, 81, 84, 95, 126, 128, *124-125*
Pyrrhura frontalis, 125, 130
Pyrrhura frontalis chiripepe, 125
Pyrrhura frontalis kriegi, 126
Pyrrhura leucotis, 126
Pyrrhura melanura, 129
Pyrrhura melanura berlepschi, 130
Pyrrhura melanura chapmani, 130
Pyrrhura melanura pacifica, 130
Pyrrhura melanura souancei, 130
Pyrrhura molinae, 130
Pyrrhura perlata, 131
Pyrrhura perlata anerythra, 132
Pyrrhura perlata coerulescens, 133
Pyrrhura perlata pseudoperlata, 133
Pyrrhura picta, 133
Pyrrhura picta amazonum, *133*, 134
Pyrrhura picta caeruleiceps, 133
Pyrrhura picta microtera, 134
Pyrrhura picta orinocensis, 134
Pyrrhura picta subandina, 134

Queen of Bavaria's Conure, 8, 25, 28, 81, 82, *93*, 94, 95
Raspberries, 38
Red-bellied Conure, 8, 64, 70, *125*, 126, 130, 131
Red currants, 38
Red-headed Conure, 92
Red-masked Conure, *92*
Roosting site, 50
Roundworm, 56
Sandsheets, 21, 55
Santarem Conure, *133*
Scaly-breasted Conure, 125
Scrambled egg, 39
Seed types, 36
Sexing, 26, 64, 84, 94, 104
Size, 17
Soaked sunflower seed, 37, 78
Soaking seed, 36
Spoon-feeding, 78
Stress, 58
Sun Conure, 8, 39, 82, 96, 97, *99*, 101
Surgical sexing, 26, 64, 95, 138
Suspended aviary, 30
Temperature, 43
Tovi Parakeet, 11, *106*, 107, 108
Treats, 41
Tui Parakeet, *109*
Uruguay, 119
Venezuela, 99, 106, 128, 130, 134
Vitamin and mineral supplements, 41
Weddell's Conure, 102
Welded mesh size, 26
White-eared Conure, *126*, 129
White-eyed Conure, *98*
White millet seed, 36
White-winged Parakeet, 11, *111*, 112
Wild foods, 38
Wing-clipping, 45
Yellow-headed Conure, 96
Yellow-winged Parakeet, 111